WAXING AND WANING

ESSAYS ON MOON KNIGHT

WAXING AND WANING

ESSAYS ON MOON KNIGHT

EDITED BY

SCOTT WEATHERLY

SEQUART ORGANIZATION   EDWARDSVILLE, ILLINOIS

Waxing and Waning: Essays on Moon Knight
edited by Scott Weatherly

First edition, November 2023, ISBN 978-1-9405-8934-3.

Cover by J-man. Book design by Julian Darius. Interior art is © its respective owners.

Published by Sequart Organization. Edited by Scott Weatherly.

For more information about other titles in this series, visit Sequart.org/books.

Contents

Foreword

by David Finch

The writers in this book have created a fantastic guidebook to Moon Knight, and if ever there was a character in need of their deep insight and historical knowledge, Moon Knight is it. He's so often misunderstood, which is understandable since he's such a difficult character to pin down. Most long-standing characters in the comic medium have gone through multiple interpretations, but Moon Knight himself is a character with multiple personalities and identities, which makes him not only a flexible vehicle for commentary on our times but also a chance for some serious introspection into our own psyche and motivations.

When I started my Moon Knight run with Charlie Huston in 2006, I knew very little at all about Moon Knight if I'm being perfectly honest. I was a huge fan of Steven Platt's very short run about a decade and a half earlier, and of Tommy Lee Edwards' interpretation more recently. I wanted to incorporate those styles into my version of the character, taking Steven's wild, over-the-top machismo, and Tommy's sense of realism to try to piece together a visual of a character that I saw as little more than Marvel's off-brand Batman. At the time, that was enough for me. Moon Knight had the potential to be a badass character, dark and brooding, and all the things that I love to draw. I was very fortunate though to have Charlie Huston's script to guide me. I learned so much more about who Moon Knight is from Charlie, and that instilled in me a deep appreciation for what a complex, original and versatile character he is.

In the years that followed, Warren Ellis took Moon Knight much further, and the Moon Knight Disney+ show turned out to be very different from the character that I knew in my run, but he was still Moon Knight, just more complex and layered. That, coupled with reading years of storytelling by Doug Moench and Bill Sienkiewicz and many others that came before, has made Moon Knight one of my favourite characters of all time.

But ultimately, I'm no scholar. Reading this book has been a revelation for me. Moon Knight works on so many levels, and the writers break down years of story to provide incredible clarity. A character with so many aliases, personalities and interpretations is a tough nut to crack for the most dedicated fan, but this book brings it all together. It tells us why he is who he is, and what it all means, all done in an approachable and entertaining way.

I'm so excited for you to read this book! In here, you'll find so much valuable insight into exactly what makes our favourite lunatic... tick. Uh, obviously I'm no writer either. So enough from me. Enjoy the journey.

All the best,
David Finch
November 2023

Introduction

by Scott Weatherly

For a character that started as a throwaway antagonist for a largely forgotten 70s monster comic, Moon Knight has come a long way. He has evolved and changed over his 45-plus-year career to become beloved by a committed fanbase. It was this fanbase that I tapped into to create this book. It's a fanbase passionate about the character but also willing to embrace, and even celebrate, the inconsistencies and ambiguities of a complex cannon that is rich with ideas.

The hugely impactful Charlie Huston and David Finch run (2006) introduced me to Moon Knight. This brought me in enough that when I spotted the title *Moon Knight* peeping out from a pile of comics in a box, sitting in a dusty corner of a second-hand book shop in the small coastal town of Whitby, I dove in to find more. I pulled about ten *Moon Knight* issues from that box. Some from the original Doug Moench run, one from *Fist of Khonshu*, and several from *Marc Spector: Moon Knight*. I read them over the next couple of days and wanted to know and read, more.

At the time the only collected editions of *Moon Knight* were three volumes of the *Essential* series. However, these only covered the earliest appearances and the Moench run. They were also rare and expensive. So, I started tracking down the original issues and building up my own collection. It took several years but I was able to complete the runs, from his first appearance in Werewolf by night #32 (1975) to the Huston / Finch run. From then on, I have collected each new run. It's a solid collection I'm really proud of and came in very useful when pulling this book together.

While I may be a big Moon Knight fan, there are others that have supported the fandom and carried the word of Khonshu to many others. At this point, I want to give a shout-out to Rey Gesmundo of the *Into the Knight* podcast, for all his support, quality content and just being a great guy. Also, the people behind *Moon Knight-core*, those people that brought us the, now infamous, Dracula nerd meme.

Figure 1: Meme created by Moon Knight-core. Image taken from *Solo Avengers* #3 (1987).

The fact that so many people were convinced that this panel came from an actual Moon Knight comic goes to show how little he is known, but also the craziness they expect from the character. He will never be in the A-list camp for Marvel, but this has become a benefit for Moon Knight and the creators that have taken him, as they have been able, to some interesting places.

While working on this book I have been given the opportunity to consider Moon Knight as a character, a concept, and a representation of Marvel Superhero comics. The first key thought that came to mind was how Moon Knight's history (up to 2023) can be broken into four phases (which seems appropriate for Marvel). During each of these phases, Moon Knight is both a representation of the times and an identifiably different character from the phase before and after.

Phase One (1975-1980) – *Finding his Feet*: This is the period from his creation to the start of his first solo run. During these years the character shifts a great deal, finding his feet as well as his look and mission. Moon Knight guest stars in several other heroes' comics and gets specials in comics like *Marvel Spotlight*. It's possible within each of these appearances to chart the development of key character elements (glider cape, personas etc.). It's only after Doug Moench and Bill Sienkiewicz defined him during the *HULK! Magazine* backups that he was able to transition and truly join the wider Marvel universe.

Phase Two (1980-1994) – *The Caped Crusader*: This phase is defined by Moon Knight being given a definitive origin story by Moench, and becoming a force for social good, as well as connecting with a wider team of people, in addition to Marlene and Frenchie. During this phase, Moon Knight is on a redemption path related to his origin and mercenary past. He is a hero working for the greater good and his battles weave from social commentary to monster of the week villains, and eventually to multi-issue story arcs. Although there is a short foray into the supernatural, it is at odds with the rest of his comics during this phase. Moench wants to use him as an exploration of social concerns, while Chuck Dixon wants to make him a caped James Bond. Also, for a character associated with the moon, he spends a lot of time in daylight.

Phase Three (1998-2012) – *Resurrection Trauma*: Phase Two ends with Moon Knight's death in *Marc Spector: Moon Knight* #60 (1994) when he sacrifices himself to save others. The new phase starts with his second death resurrection in *Resurrection Wars* (1998). The odd thing about this short series is that there is no confirmed explanation given for his return from the dead. This leads to a depiction of Moon Knight struggling with his identity; the violent (*secret*) avenger of the night, righteous hero doing good, or Hollywood producer, as he bounces around North and Central America. All the time dealing with Khonshu's demands for adulation and blood. In addition, his mental illness comes to the fore, finally being defined by taking on different Avenger personalities.

Phase Four (2014-present) – *They Call Me Mister Knight*: Starting with the Ellis run (2014) we find that Moon Knight is working on himself and is a confident and violent vigilante. Following this we get a more psychological Moon Knight, finally dealing with his own childhood and military trauma, and managing his relationship with Khonshu. He is embracing who he is and how that makes him good at what he does. This has allowed him to keep the darker edge that came from his resurrection trauma, but able to build a team and a mission, similar to his time as the *caped crusader*. This is the iteration that has caught the imagination of the comic audience the most and while Moon Knight is still dealing with psychological and supervillain issues, he has started to work his way up the superhero hierarchy.

Throughout all of these, though, one consistent element of the character is his inability to be at peace with himself. Despite everything he has done in therapy and through his adventures, Moon Knight understands that he is dangerous to be around and can never, in his mind at least, make up for the suffering he has left in his wake.

This highlights the duality the character struggles with. He clearly wanted to be a figure of hope and redemption but has steadily migrated to a darker place. He has become side-lined by the central superhero community, while still being a hero to a vulnerable group of night travellers.

This is interesting when we consider a character that is so heavily associated with the moon and its tinges of the supernatural. Aside from being a rock that is trapped in an orbit around the earth, the moon has been a fascinating part of cultures and mysticism, going back beyond the ancient Egyptians that recognised Khonshu.

The moon is the light in the dark. A shining light giving some solace from the creeping darkness. A lone beacon that prevents us from being completely engulfed in the night. This is the position that Moon Knight now holds in the Marvel Universe. Most heroes exist in a daylight world of heroics and adventures. Even the Punisher is often depicted within that daylight world, living among the Avengers and those that are accepted by the wider world. Moon Knight has always struggled to be a part of that. Even during the caped crusader phase, when he joined the West Coast Avengers and was part of their *wacky* adventures, he was at odds with them. To such an extent that he left the group, breaking relationships that would not be repaired for years.

Even during the most hero-friendly phase Moon Knight stood apart from the rest of the superhero community. He shares and reflects the light of these heroes, but he is much more comfortable as a figure in the darkness. A light that will stand up for those that have no choice but to travel at night. He states that he is the one you see coming, and while this has a good ring to it, there is more to it.

To take the idea of the moon and mysticism further we can consider the position the moon takes in the Tarot, as this highlights further parallels with Moon Knight. The moon card presents the moon as a partial face of the sun, yet still in the night. This face looks down on a dark landscape between two towers, on either side of a river. Moon Knight is the same figure. A night creature reflecting the light of the sun into the night, a beacon illuminating the landscape for those that travel its paths. Moreover, the two towers represent the worlds Moon Knight passes between. The regular world, the mainstream heroes, and regular people. The other is the world of hidden entities and the supernatural. He is not wholly of either, but he can walk between them and kick ass in each.

In addition to this, the two towers can be seen to represent the two parts of Moon Knight. There is the hero, his desire to do good and be a figure of hope. The other is his rage and ease with violence. He has worked from both towers and been successful, but he is most successful when he is able to bridge the gap between them.

Despite the aforementioned phases, Moon Knight's print history is a little convoluted. A mix of shorter runs, as well as combining new and legacy issue numbering. To make things clearer for each of the essays in this book, I have created the below table to show how the volumes are referenced.

Volume	Title	Issues	Years
1	Moon Knight	38	1980-1983
2	Moon Knight: Fist of Khonshu	6	1985
3	Moon Knight: Resurrection Wars	4	1998
4	Moon Knight: High Strangers	4	1999
5	Moon Knight	30	2006-2009
6	Moon Knight	12	2011-2012
7	Moon Knight	17	2014-2015
8	Moon Knight	14	2016-2017
9	Moon Knight	13	2017-2018
10	Moon Knight	-	2021-present
N/A	Marc Spector: Moon Knight	60	1989-1994
N/A	Vengeance of the Moon Knight	10	2009-2010

Moving from the character, I want to state how thrilled I am by the contributions that have been submitted for this book. The essays contain fantastic analysis as well as some incredibly personal insights. However, there are three things that I want to address before you read any further.

First and foremost, there is an essay in this book that discusses and analyses the six-issue run known as *From the Dead*, written by Warren Ellis. Understanding what Ellis did, I thought hard about if and how to address these issues. At first, I thought about not including them at all but after discussing the essay topics with the contributors it become obvious to me that they are key to the history and development of the character. Also, as highlighted in the phases above, this run is a clear starting point for phase four and has had a large impact on the character and his canon.

Therefore, I decided that I would take on the run myself. I want to be clear: no one involved in this book condones or supports the actions of Warren Ellis, but I decided to include this analysis as I felt it was important to the character.

The second is in regards to the interview with Chuck Dixon. While working on this book, it was highlighted to me that he holds certain views that have offended and alienated people in the past. We do not endorse or support these views. However, I felt it was important to keep the interview, since he is a contributor to Moon Knight lore and the run he started (*Marc Spector: Moon Knight*) has not had much told about its history.

The third item to mention is the essay by Leyna Vincent, an alter of the Douglas J. Vincent system. Leyna is candid about her experiences as part of a dissociative system and a Moon Knight fan. I will admit that when we first corresponded, I was unsure if this would be the right thing to include. Having read the essay and spoken with Leyna, I am so pleased to have her essay as part of this collection. It gives a perspective that is vital to the analysis of Moon Knight as well as how society approaches psychological conditions.

With that said, please take a seat and welcome to the Midnight Mission.

Phases of Moon Knight: A Glimpse at a Character's Improvisational History

by Jason D. DeHart

I was 9 or 10 years old when I first encountered Moon Knight. I don't have a clear and distinct memory of seeing him in a comic book, per se, although I might have run across him in an issue of *The West Coast Avengers*. This was a run that was out around the time I began reading comics and I have a vague recollection of an issue with Tigra. I do remember clearly seeing the character rendered on a 1992 Impel Marvel Universe trading card. The sweep of Moon Knight's cloak extended out of the half-circle as the hooded character glared at the viewer with a darkened face. The urban landscape behind Moon Knight serves as a quick look into the world of a character who worked across the streets and rooftops of some mythical, yet very grounded metropolis.

I knew next to nothing about Marc Spector, his origin and complexity, his powers, or his rogue's gallery, but I was instantly fascinated by his design. My mind immediately drew parallels to Jim Valentino's *ShadowHawk* series, which was popular at that time, and of course, to Batman, a common, and yet incomplete, comparison to the character. What I did not know in the glimpse was that Moon Knight had a long, convoluted history and that this was merely a look at one impression of the character, with many more possibilities to come.

Christie[1] pointed to the lesser-known nature of the character and so it may still be the case that many comics readers have not kept track of Moon Knight's twists and turns over the decades.

In this chapter, I trace an incomplete history of Moon Knight from his origins as a villain to his heroic reestablishment. Also, the complicated series of identities that the character has assumed in more recent years, and finally to where he is at the time of this writing, a potential new vehicle for audiences as part of the Marvel Cinematic Universe. While a full portrait of each iteration of the character is not possible in this space, the linkages between storytellers and the juxtaposition of story elements provide an intriguing mosaic for examining the character in more detail across multiple incarnations.

Other characters retain essential elements with few changing features, fixed in the same static characterization. Moon Knight however is different, he is a character whose nature is at odds with itself, often with delightful narrative consequences and unique improvisations on the part of the storytellers who visit his urban world.

Villain

Moon Knight's seminal appearance in 1975's *Werewolf by Night* #32 features Marc Spector as a secondary character and, in fact, as a villain whose costume and equipment are provided to him by *The Committee*. The shadow organization enlisted him in his capacity as a mercenary. Indeed, his superhero identity is given to him as he is told to introduce himself as Moon Knight. Spector says, "Pretty stupid name – but it'll do as far as you're concerned,"[2] and relinquishes any agency that he possibly has as a figure on a mission.

The reader first encounters Moon Knight on the cover. He is engaged in combat with the Werewolf, four of his soon-to-be iconic crescent moons penetrating his enemy. Elements of lycanthrope lore make their way into Moon Knight's attire, from his silver-laden gloves with spikes to the moon that decorates his chest. These adornments would later be co-opted into a more focused origin story for the character, taking on new meanings. In this first

---

[1] Christie, C. "Sane superheroes mental distress in the gutters of Moon Knight." *Uncanny Bodies*. Penn State University Press, 2019. Pages 59-78.
[2] "The Stalker Called Moon Knight," *Werewolf by Night* Vol. 1 #32 (1975). By Doug Moench, Gil Kane, and Phil Rache.

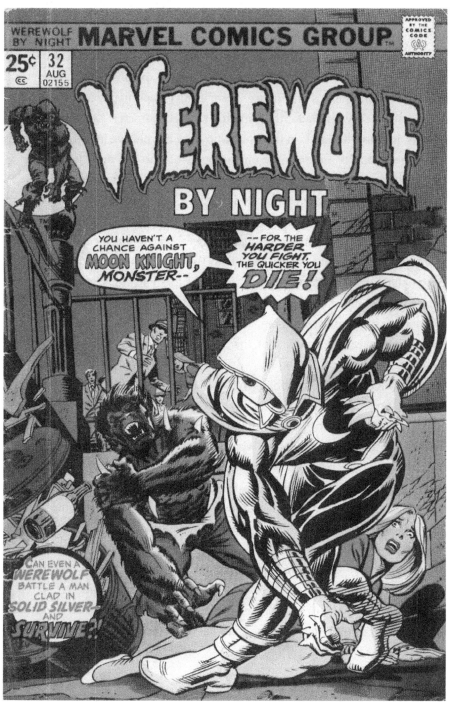

Moon Knight in his very first iteration, from his first appearance in *Werewolf by Night* #32 (1975).

appearance, however, their existence is tied to the Werewolf character, Jack Russell.

His tools are described as "silver, of course, and shaped in a crescent -- sort of like the moon,"[3] drawing to mind the imagery of lore. This supernatural aspect of Moon Knight's affordances for narrative is perhaps part of why he is often associated with Blade, the vampiric Marvel character. Marc Spector, for his part, is a stated skeptic in the book who does not believe in werewolves but has taken a job, as a mercenary on the hunt for one. He does not bother to question but faces new-found danger with an unchecked determination.

Moon Knight is described as "Fast, brutal, and armed with everything to produce a scream" and also as a "weirdo".[4] The character's first appearance, then, is as a figure, directed to attack and defeat a mythological being, and as an outsider. This mythological sensibility would continue as the character progressed. Even though the use of the unreliable narrator convention in Jeff Lemire's 2016 run, in which elements of legend are called into question as delusions or realized encounters.

It should also be noted, that the "cestus," or glove, is described as one "worn by gladiators in the arena,"[5] an element that would make its way into Moon Knight's characterization, as a former boxer and bruiser. This forms part of the continued outsider/loner quality of the character, along with a relentless nature, a "silver lightning" that "wouldn't quit."[6]

We see this adaptation and weaving of elements across Moon Knight's multiple variations, retaining some aspects of the character while transposing others. Even when faced with the last issue of a run, or transitioning to a new mythology, situation, or even costume, some pieces endure, only to find themselves re-rendered in a new context. Other elements – from Spector's wavering belief, the covering of his face to obscure his identity, to full-out searches for self – shift from run to run. This results in jarring explorations of existential crisis, bringing depth, pathos, and intellect to the character.

Moon Knight initially appears as a villain in the follow-up issue (*Werewolf by Night* #33), completing the story and being given partial redemption. In his

---

[3] Ibid.
[4] Ibid.
[5] Ibid.
[6] Ibid.

subsequent appearances, he starts to be reconfigured as a more complete character. This time, a hero with an origin not tied to The Committee, a list of enemies, with the return of his sidekick, Frenchie. This sidekick/support character's history also proves complicated as he is later envisioned as a member of the LGBTQ community, serving Marc Spector because of romantic interest.

What is striking about these early appearances of Moon Knight are the elements that remain and are co-opted when he later appears as a heroic figure. His mercenary past, or hero/villain for hire premise, allows an outside bidder to give Moon Knight a mission. While the mercenary element remains, this will become the darker part of the character, something he will try to escape and redeem by becoming his own man. The act of choosing a costume and name, which is usually tied to the specific origin of the character, and so intrinsically personal, is left to The Committee. This is revised to meet the expected criteria when it is Khonshu that brings him back from the dead. The name and costume now form a part of a confused belief system.

This outline of an emerging character later provided threads from which creators Doug Moench and Don Perlin spun a new identity when Marv Wolfman and Len Wein drew on the character for the *Marvel Spotlight*[7] arc.

Heroic Figure

Before his own title, Moon Knight was cast as a background/backup player in *The Defenders*, a kind of street-corner-style take on the Avengers. This arc results in a dynamic of a loner figure and support player in a larger cast that allowed readers to know the character better, gaining some traction before his solo run. Moon Knight, here, is part of a community that includes commercial mainstays like Spider-Man and Hulk. Alongside this positioning with the wider Marvel narrative, Moon Knight's presence and story arc solidifies his origin and familiar relationships, as well as his romantic entanglement with Marlene and his relationship with the sidekick character, Frenchie. As part of a sprawling interaction, Moon Knight was given the chance to live and breathe, develop, and become, so that he could emerge and carry his own title. It is the kind of

---

[7] "The Crushing Conquer Lord!" *Marvel Spotlight* Vol. 1 #28-29 (1976). By Doug Moench, Don Perlin, and I Vartanoff.

commercial linking that exists across media and allows lesser-known characters to hit the market successfully on the heels of characters with greater exposure.

When Doug Moench returns to the character in the first issue, the story begins with Marc Spector as a mercenary once more, a "soldier-for-hire"[8] archetype that perhaps exists to quell his previous role as a villain. We can, perhaps, excuse this former villainy as a mere mission, or else exclude it from the new canon of the character entirely. Spector is accomplished in his work as a killer, but uncomfortable with the violence, and the reader is introduced to a villain by the second panel in the book. Of course, Moon Knight is never without some sense of characteristic darkness or, as Jonason et al. termed it, a "Dark Triad," consisting of "subclinical narcissism, psychopathy, and Machiavellianism."[9] While these researchers point to the antiheroic nature of Batman and Tony Stark, Marc Spector/Moon Knight is arguably a more comprehensive example, given his inclination for extreme life-threatening methods, his brutal past, and his navigation of multiple personalities.

How to cast such a character in a positive light? Heroes are often defined by their villains, and even a frightening figure can be recast as an antihero if the right antagonist is included to highlight the redeeming qualities of the newly found hero. Here, the reader meets Raoul Bushman for the first time. A character that will emerge and reemerge, even conquering death behind his ghostly facial tattoo. Bushman's face is "tattooed into a mask of death" and describes himself as "an almost mythical figure of terror."[10] This can be seen as an ironic link to Moon Knight's original appearance, battling a similar mythical character associated with fear in the form of the werewolf. Perhaps Moon Knight is destined to take on the nightmare characters of horror lore that other characters only meet every so often in between more grounded battles.

Marc Spector distances himself from the identity of the *murderer* by suggesting that, while Bushman is malevolent, Spector has a moral compass,

---

[8] "The Macabre Moon Knight." *Moon Knight* Vol. 1 #1 (Nov 1980). By Doug Moench, Bill Sienkiewicz, and B. Sharen.

[9] Jonason, P. K.; Webster, G. D.; Schmitt, D. P.; Li, N. P.; & Crysel, L. "The antihero in popular culture: Life history theory and the dark triad personality traits." *Review of General Psychology* Vol. 2 #16. American Psychological Association, 2012. Pages 192-199.

[10] "The Macabre Moon Knight." *Moon Knight* Vol. 1 #1 (Nov 1980). By Doug Moench, Bill Sienkiewicz, and B. Sharen.

pushing him to the side of good. He highlights that he is a professional soldier, not a killer. While the act of killing in these terms can be debated (and is in later runs), Spector wants it to be perceived as transactional rather than emotional. Therefore, he can transition to the role of protector without having to address any *evil* characteristics. Whether when protecting Marlene and her father, or when he is returned from the dead and takes on the role of Moon Knight.

Here, Spector is stepping into a new archetypal role, yet he is still interwoven with his former role as a servant to an outside source. Only now it is the Egyptian god Khonshu. To what degree Spector is influenced by Khonshu is a matter of interpretation. As suggested previously, it is often considered easy to align Moon Knight with characters like Batman or Spawn, but the heroic transition narrative arc is arguably divergent from these. Spector's transition from conflicted soldier to superhero takes place as he suffers the wrath of the desert and perishes, ending his own story.

At this moment Marc Spector mercenary for hire dies and is reborn as an agent for the Egyptian god, Khonshu. The nature of this moment is cast in doubt as Moench tells us, "Perhaps it is a natural phenomenon which causes Marc Spector's heart to resume throbbing...perhaps it is something else."[11] This dissonance between the natural and supernatural takes on fascinating turns through the character's narrative trajectory, but more on this later.

In his moment of revival, Spector sits upright and identifies a statue of Khonshu as "the taker of vengeance" and "a figure of terror."[12] Spector is not aware of how he has attained this knowledge, but immediately wraps himself in a white cloak, saying "I'm a ghost now... a spectre of the moon... the moon's knight of vengeance – and I've got work to do."[13] There is the wordplay with Spector's name as *spectre*, a prophecy from his family name of whom he was destined to become. The notion of the figure of dread and terror is well situated in the mythology of Moon Knight. With characters like Werewolf by Night and Bushman existing in a similar world of existential fear. I also note the use of gothic and dreadful figures in Moench's work outside of *Moon Knight*.[14]

---

[11] Ibid.

[12] Ibid.

[13] Ibid.

[14] *Batman/Dracula: Red Rain* (DC Comics, 1992). By Doug Moench, Kelley Jones, and Les Dorscheid.

Khonshu, or Khons, is indeed the Egyptian god of the moon and is adorned with a cobra hood, similar to the kind of hood that Marc Spector takes up.[15] In a moment of tragic irony, the reluctant mercenary is recast as a hero at odds with life and death, carrying out the will of an Egyptian god with or without his consent[16]. According to Zachary, Khonshu is "one of the Celestial Heliopolis, a cache of powerful beings worshipped by the ancient Egyptians. Formerly the mentor to Horus and the rival to Seth, Khonshu's motivations have always appeared mysterious to the human eye - even once the being chose a human avatar in the form of Moon Knight."[17] There is an element of mystery from the very beginning, suggested by the choice of Spector as his avatar at the moment of death. Also, Khonshu does indeed have an unclear agenda, initially unseen, but explored in storylines to come.

Rather than being content with a singular secret identity, Spector goes on to obtain three new personas: retaining Marc Spector, as well as millionaire Steven Grant, and street-smart cabbie Jake Lockley.[18] These identities assemble and work together to form a support system for Spector's new role as Moon Knight, presented in full costume and "continuing the mission begun in the pharaoh's tomb."[19] Moench, in an interview with the *Into the Knight Podcast* in 2019,[20] pointed to the practical needs of the character to become aware of moments when danger would occur, or when he might be needed. Moench expressed frustration with the moment in typical superhero storylines when a character stumbles upon a crime in progress and just happens to seize the moment to perform a heroic feat. In contrast, the Jake Lockley persona serves as a "logical way for this guy to practice his craft," while Steven Grant's resources provide the necessary foundation for equipment, global travel, and other needs. Though logical, later writers would expand on these multiple

---

[15] Britannica www.britannica.com/topic/Khons

[16] Zachary, Brandon. "Avengers: Who is Khonshu, the god of Moon Knight?" Comic Book Resources, 2020. www.cbr.com/avengers-who-is-khonshu-the-god-of-moon-knight/

[17] Ibid.

[18] "The Macabre Moon Knight." *Moon Knight* Vol. 1 #1 (Nov 1980). By Doug Moench, Bill Sienkiewicz, and B. Sharen.

[19] Ibid.

[20] "Retrospective: Doug Moench Interview." *Into the Moon Knight Podcast*, 2019. www.youtube.com/watch?v=t4yLD1bSMJw

identities as a diagnosed dissociative disorder, adding another layer to the questions of control for Moon Knight.

The first issue closes its narrative circle with a further confrontation between Moon Knight and Bushman. However, we need to ask, whose mission is Moon Knight on. Is this a character of natural origins who merely resuscitated at the moment, or a man now imbued with the power of an ancient moon god? While Moon Knight tangles with ideas of agency and morality, the invisible threads of the narrative always suggest the possibility of a larger chess game, one the hero is never fully aware of. It is, from a philosophical perspective, one of the features of the character which unites him so universally with the human experience. With the uncertain mixture of motive, intention, and realization, are we really in charge of our own stories?

Avenger(?)

So, does the Moon Knight character get invited to the party with other heroes in the Marvel universe? According to Zachary,[21] Moon Knight does join the West Coast Avengers. His entrance into the team in the late 1980s is at the characteristic behest of his godly benefactor, Khonshu. The god then utilizes Spector's membership to engage in battle with his rival, Seth. The result of this enlistment does not fall in Moon Knight's favour.

The alliance, officially formed in *The West Coast Avengers #21*, is often uneasy. Moon Knight is more closely aligned with The Defenders or The Punisher, characters of a similar leaning toward violence and grittier storylines. While Moon Knight's narrative allows for cyborgs and mystical beings, he is also at home in the bloody world of hand-to-hand combat. Through the narrative arc, Moon Knight runs afoul of Thor and severs his membership with the team.

Before ending this affiliation, Moon Knight's relationship with the team is complicated by a love affair and disagreements over his more extreme methods. As well as entanglements with other problems that arise within the team, including the abuse of Mockingbird by Phantom Rider. Moon Knight's loyalty to the female character, even when she is cast out, is an alignment between methods. As the team leader, Hawkeye disagrees with Mockingbird's

---

[21] Zachary, Brandon. "Avengers: Who is Khonshu, the god of Moon Knight?" Comic Book Resources, 2020. www.cbr.com/avengers-who-is-khonshu-the-god-of-moon-knight/

complicity in the death of Phantom Rider. This storyline also lends support to the notion that female characters are often portrayed as devices in comics whose abuse is used to shape the male characters' narratives...

Spector and Khonshu part ways in the storyline, as the Egyptian god's true control of the situation in gaining affiliation with the team, is revealed.[22] This brings a resolution, at least in part, to the mystery of the level of control Khonshu has over Marc. This conflict of control in their relationship is revisited in later volumes. In addition to this, Moon Knight would return to a covert version of the Avengers, in a 2010 run entitled *Secret Avengers*.

His allegiance is never complete and while he is included in these teams it is only on the roster of splinter groups. Also, often while being at odds with the rest of the team over his methods. Marc Spector consistently marks himself apart from the group and is willing to take measures that many other heroes in the Marvel lineup would consider unethical.

In short, Moon Knight does not always play well with others and, while helpful at times, has complicated relationships and motivations that place him at odds with the more morally clear-cut members of the team. In fact, during the Jason Aaron run on Avengers (2018) Moon Knight defeated the Avengers team in the name of Khonshu, under the belief that it was the only way to defend the earth from a larger threat. This was however corrupted for Khonshu to take over the world. While this was resolved and Moon Knight is back on the streets, it once again puts him at odds with the team and highlights his potential to be controlled by the manipulative Egyptian god.

Rogue

Iterations in the 1970s and 1990s explored Moon Knight's darker tendencies. These have been expanded upon during the 2000s and 2010s, including a slow transition towards being more horror-centric. For this chapter of the character's journey, I will focus on the opening arc of Charlie Huston's run, "The Bottom."[23]

---

[22] This takes place on *West Coast Avengers* #41 and strips Moon Knight of his supernatural powers. This is demonstrated by the destruction of his golden accessories and is topped off by a discussion between Marc and Khonshu, in which Khonshu leaves Marc to be just a man, representing Khonshu on Earth.
[23] "The Bottom." *Moon Knight* Vol. 5 #1-5 (2006). By Charlie Huston, David Finch, and Frank D'Armata.

Charlie Huston's treatment of the character in his 2006 run gives a ragged and tattered look to a figure that once looked pristine. The earlier depictions that make Moon Knight appear ready to jump into the line-up of clean and neat Avenger types are replaced by a Punisher-style approach to inner conflict expressed through his outward appearance.

When we are reintroduced to the character it is revealed that he has recently killed Bushman. In fact, he removed his enemy's face. Spector is beaten by this event and his turmoil is evident. Giving himself over the more violent and fearful elements of his character has taken its toll. This fall from grace is presented through David Finch's pencils and Danny Miki's inks.

There is a sudden new depth and darkness given to the urban landscape first encountered in the 1992 trading card introduction to this character. A sequence of five panels is stacked up in uneven juxtaposition, taking the reader from the tops of buildings to street levels, across pipes, and along power lines. This opening scene operates as an introduction to a new status quo. One that is built upon by subsequent titles, as I will explore shortly. Gone are the whimsical colours and trappings of *The West Coast Avengers*, replaced by grime and blood.

Moon Knight intones, "Someone has to do this...the other guys. The world savers. They got their own jobs to do. A giant monster pops out of the ground in the financial district? Call the Fantastic Four. Magneto trying to wipe out the human race? X-Men on the job,"[24] and this litany continues, again noting the divide between this character's worldview and that of many of the other Marvel heroes. Presenting this contrast and divergence we can see that Moon Knight is again an outsider who is sometimes welcomed, yet mostly *othered*. Moon Knight exists, seeming to thrive, in these fragments. When the reader reaches the bottom of page two, a shootout between cars at street level is depicted, before a splash page introduces Moon Knight once more. He sweeps in, saying "Someone has to do the *fun* stuff."[25] As this statement makes clear, he enjoys his work, and he is *not* one of those "other guys."

It is here that Moon Knight stretches and breathes as a contemporary character. Balancing blood and madness with death with exhilaration in a

---

[24] "The Bottom: Chapter One." Moon Knight Vol. 5 #1 (2006). By Charlie Huston, David Finch, and Frank D'Armata.
[25] Ibid.

universe of larger-than-life figures, he is also larger than death, depression, and despair. Other characters have full feature runs where their demise is depicted and their journey back from the grave is a publishing event with spectacle. For Moon Knight, such a spectacle is positioned alongside these street-level encounters and is just another moment in a long history of resurrections. He is a character who is at home in space, in a broken-down apartment, in the sands of Egypt, or at the gates of hell.

Contrasting with this street-level take on the character we have the presence of technology. In the opening book of the Huston run as we glimpse the Moon-copter, reintroducing the reader to Frenchie. Yet we are to learn that Frenchie has suffered along with Marc since that horrific event. There is also a sense of urban horror and decay to the character here that is only hinted at in earlier iterations. This is woven in with the science fiction sensibility that keeps Moon Knight's vigilante escapades in the comics world of billionaire heroes, who use their funds to purchase advanced equipment, somehow completing these transactions in seclusion.

We are exposed to violence, human affection, urban battlefield trauma, and prescription drug abuse before we see Marc Spector as a fallen hero. He is crumpled at the feet of a Khonshu statue, pleading, "...please, let me be a hero again."[26] The vacillation between identities, from human to superhuman, from hero to villain, is at the core of this arc. Moon Knight engages in violent and unethical tactics that would seem vastly out of place in a Spider-Man, or most other Marvel characters, comics. Once more, the push and pull of what defines this character are exposed, exemplified by the character design, illustrating Spector's complexity and depth.

The genre-bending aspect of Moon Knight draws upon the hero narrative, horror archetypes, and science fiction stories, highlighting an evident contrast to the traditional vigilante story. These varying aspects of the character are presented as Marc Spector begins to lie to himself later on in the arc. His role as a mercenary, millionaire, working-class man, and malevolent hero are presented in the comic. Both the reader and the arc's antagonists are shown a selection of images of Spector in a military uniform, a formal suit, modest street clothing, and finally the traditional hooded costume. These images serve the story as exposition and as a visual reminder for the reader that Moon Knight is

---

[26] Ibid.

notable for his departure from the binary secret identity story type of most characters. He is, in fact, a composite character working to make sense of his own identity, as the reader travels with him on this complex existential journey.

Huston and Finch present a storyline that is propulsive, driving, bloody, and visceral. It draws on the combat-worn nature of the character, re-casting him as a modern Prometheus. He is stitched together from fragments of himself, only to disassemble his enemies. In this arc and the wider run, his path to redemption is bloody and near impossible. He strives to stand back up only to find the nemesis figure, Raoul Bushman waiting. Yet this return itself is a twisted reality, crafted by Khonshu and the god's need for violent subjugation and worship.

Huston pushes Moon Knight up the ladder of redemption, only for him to have to face another consequence of his past. The tattered remains of his external design, a representation of the guilt of past actions. This constant struggle is a further depiction of the chess game between Marc and Khonshu for control, as well as for the need to fulfil a destiny, whether as a hero or the violent avatar of an ancient deity.

Wandering Assassin

In a similar, yet arguably slightly less visceral vein, author Charlie Hurwitz's take on Moon Knight operates in a street-level world of criminal reckoning and a supernatural universe of extraordinary beings. This is the same thematic tension that would have made Christopher Nolan's take on Batman a hard sell in the DC Extended Universe approach to film that was attempted in 2016 and 2017.

Yet, for Moon Knight, the two worlds work. The reader is again introduced to the hero through a street-level encounter. This time riding a motorcycle and taking on some common thugs. At the end of the first issue, the superhuman character, Sentry, descends and asks our hero the central question of his comic journey; "Who do you think you are...?"[27] For Moon Knight, there is no simple answer. He has just provided an internal subjective narration, across multiple panels, examining his prior sins. Explaining his current attempt at seeking transformation and redemption for his prior violence. Khonshu, now a small

---

[27] "Shock and Awe, Part 1." *Vengeance of the Moon Knight* #1 (2009). By Gregg Hurwitz, Jerome Opeña, and Dan Brown.

figure sitting on Moon Knight's shoulder, attempts to push him to violent actions, which Moon Knight resists. The dynamic of Khonshu's appearance here is a mirror of Spector's resistance to violence and worshipful subjugation. The god is reduced, having not been sated by the violence of the titular hero.

There is no such resistance in Warren Ellis's 2014 take on the character. In his six-issue run, collected as *From the Dead*,[28] Moon Knight has expanded upon his traditional costume of hood and armour and introduces a new persona, Mr Knight. Dressed in a white suit and close-fitting cowl that covers his face, he makes an instant impact. The costume is more down-to-earth, more tailored to reality, and the missions that Moon Knight takes are one-issue storylines in which some threat emerges, and our hero takes mercenary turns, eliminating his enemies through any violence necessary.

Moon Knight is insurmountable in these stories, deftly engaging his enemies in combat, as both a victorious and vicious figure.

Tortured Soul

However, the question remains: who, indeed, does Marc Spector think he is?

On a penultimate note, before I discuss what might be next in this character's world, I want to address Jeff Lemire's treatment of the character in the *Lunatic* storyline (2016-2017). The psychological tensions of Marc Spector's multiple identities are fully displayed, and the character is featured in a straight-jacket ensemble on the collected edition's cover. Moench introduced a sense of mystery in the character, with a balance between the natural and supernatural. Assigning three identities for the hero to travel across. In his run, Lemire takes up this mythology, returns to Spector's childhood, and imagines that the origins of the character began long before his exploits as a mercenary. Khonshu, in this storyline, was there all along, in some form, and would later beckon Spector to a closer relationship. So, to that end, does Lemire suggest that Khonshu exists as a separate entity, or as a figment of Spector's fractured imagination?

---

[28] *Moon Knight: From the Dead* (2014). By Warren Ellis, Declan Shalvey and Jordie Bellaire.

The interpretation, again, is a matter of debate. I myself lean toward the inclusion of mythology as a central element of the character, a kind of celestial interplay with humanity's psyche.

Spector is portrayed as a tragic, yet ultimately heroic, figure from birth, whose sensing of an Egyptian deity in his life is left to the reader to determine as a reality or as an illusion concocted by a potentially dangerous mind. Spector's world, at times, is rendered upside down in comic panels that have to be flipped to be read upright. Lemire questions these driving forces, these places of reality, and ultimately leaves us with a narrative that has some threads that remain unresolved. Spector, in the end, has threads that are left but positions himself as a being who has directed some agency toward his survival, establishing his sanity even if the world doubts him.

Media Fixture

At the time of this writing, the Moon Knight Disney Plus series is filming in Budapest, Hungary, and the next steps for this character remain to be seen. A new comic series has recently debuted from the creative team of writer Jed MacKay and artist Alessandro Cappuccio, with the tagline "His Mission…Is Justice!"[29] In imagery that brings to mind the opening of both the Huston and Hurwitz storylines, Moon Knight is again depicted in a street-level tussle involving an automobile accident at the outset of the first issue. The character appears as an imposing figure on page 8, stating, "This is my territory. This is my congregation. This is my mission. I'm the Moon Knight." In this one statement, the reader is reminded of the ground that Moon Knight usually haunts, and of how this terrain can shift based on the needs of the narrative. The elements of sacramental/mythological character are intimated in the use of the word "congregation," while the loss of agency and mercenary nature of the character are comprised in the word "mission." Spector is again a spectre, giving warnings to whoever is wise enough to listen, and dealing out violence to those who refuse to hear and heed.

---

[29] "The Mission." *Moon Knight* Vol. 10 #1 (2021). By Jed MacKay, Alessandro Cappuccio, and Rachelle Rosenburg.

While excitement grows for the show, there is also pushback against Oscar Isaac's casting, as some fans called for a Jewish actor to portray the role.[30] This first 2021 issue features Moon Knight referring to himself as the descendant of a rabbi, connecting with this ancestry once more. Again, there is the distinction between the person that Marc Spector was and the heroic impulse that might help him more neatly fit into the world of more polished heroes. Moon Knight says, "Don't sanitize the facts on *my* account. I was a bad man who did bad things to people in foreign countries for money,"[31] and the reader is again reminded of the Bushman nemesis, always lurking at the corners of the story. By the end of the issue, the clean and polished figure directly speaks to his dark corners and splinters his allegiance once more: "Unless I kill all of you right now. And I can. And I will. I'm not Spider-man. I'm Moon Knight. And I don't die." The character's promise certainly seems clear and accurate, given his longevity, narrative innovations, and the soon-to-come live-action depiction he will receive.

It is unclear at this point how Moon Knight will factor in as a newly minted cinematic character. In truth, I have longed to see an actor take up Moon Knight's multiple personalities and have been intrigued by the possibilities of visually representing the mystical aspects of the storyline. As I read Lemire's issues, my excitement grew. It is with some skepticism that I now imagine Moon Knight appearing on the bombastic battlefield of a Joss Whedon-style Marvel adventure, dropping quips and earning slick nicknames from other characters who humorously point out the narrative tensions of such a complex character.

This is not to suggest that other characters in the Marvel Cinematic Universe have not been depicted with intriguing duality. An example of how Marc Spector might make his way into this larger storyline may exist in Mark Ruffalo's portrayal of Bruce Banner/The Hulk. Ruffalo is an actor with nuance and range who has made the psychological dynamic of his dual character evident in his performance in ways that weave into the fabric of other characters' worlds, sometimes with humour and sometimes with pathos. He is

---

[30] Martin, Michileen. "Things Fans Want to See in Moon Knight." Looper, 2021. www.looper.com/447049/things-fans-want-to-see-in-moon-knight/

[31] "The Mission." *Moon Knight* Vol. 10 #1 (2021). By Jed MacKay, Alessandro Cappuccio, and Rachelle Rosenburg.

reluctant when we first meet him and questions his place as part of a larger team. Later, he deals with fissures in his ability to transform back and forth before ultimately deciding that his accident did have a purpose, seemingly settling him into a resolved place between identities. The human and monster are conjoined - but what remains next, even for this character, has yet to be explored as he grieves Natasha Romanoff's death.

Similarly, the mystical and otherworldly characters featured in James Gunn's *Guardians of the Galaxy* have been digitally rendered toe-to-toe with the likes of Robert Downey, Jr.'s Tony Stark/Iron Man and other characters in the series - seemingly without much of a hitch. And who would have thought that such a pairing could be executed well on the screen?

So, in the final analysis, I leave my skepticism aside with hopes that the character will be honoured in some way while noting a moment in which Marvel has had (and perhaps has squandered) the opportunity to feature a Jewish character in a prominent and quite layered role. Time will tell, and the dynamic fabric of the character will nevertheless be an interesting addition to the print and visual media landscape to come. Through this essay, I have traced Moon Knight's many turns, from being a secondary and lesser character who was dropped into another character's storyline as a villain of the week, to being the central hero. From there, Moon Knight's violence and juxtaposed desire to stray from violence contribute to his improvisational nature, as well as his presentation across multiple identities. From his ragged appearance as a figure of terror to the movement between reality and dream-vision in Lemire's treatment of the character, Moon Knight stands out as a unique hero, not quite at home with his own heroism and certainly not at peace with the mythological origins of his powers.

He is dreadful, delightful, and an always-exciting character to encounter as new authors and artists probe his possibilities.

The God on Your Shoulder

by Zach Katz

Saying that Marc Spector and the god he worships, Khonshu, the Egyptian god of the moon, have a strained relationship would be an understatement. For much of the character's publication history, Khonshu's existence was in question. Some of Spector's supporting cast assumed that the moon god was a delusion, resulting from Marc's near-death experience, combined with his Dissociative Identity Disorder. Others, however, believed Khonshu was real. Spector himself has walked on both sides of the issue, from believing that Khonshu was a product of his imagination, to wishing that was the case.

Moon Knight's early adventures place the focus on him dealing with normal, human criminals. Although there are hints in several issues that Khonshu is real and has an active influence over Spector's life, or Grant's since the Steven Grant persona seems to act as the primary during this era. Doug Moench frequently implies that Khonshu is nothing more than coincidence and Spector's own belief. However, this status quo changes immediately after Moench's tenure on the series, with Khonshu being confirmed as explicitly real and Moon Knight's adventures taking on a more supernatural tone. This change continued in the short-lived second Moon Knight series,[1] which confirmed, at least for Marc, that Khonshu was indeed real after he gained a new suit and weapons from the moon god's cult. Although other gods or mythical figures, such as Thor and Hercules, were active in Marvel Comics during this period, it took a significant amount of time for the rest of Moon Knight's supporting cast to realize that Khonshu was real, rather than a manifestation of Marc's poor mental health. In modern stories, Marc Spector no longer has to wonder if his god is real but is instead forced to deal with Khonshu's attempts to exert influence over him.

Rather than one being a divine benefactor, and the other being a priest, the relationship between Khonshu and Moon Knight during this period is adversarial. Khonshu constantly attempts to manipulate and taunt Spector to drive the character to follow his orders. Despite this, Marc still feels indebted to the moon god, only later changing his mind while attempting to act more *heroic*.

Jeff Lemire and Greg Smallwood's 2016 run with the character complicated the history between Spector and Khonshu by simultaneously placing Khonshu in a directly antagonistic role and introducing new history between the two, stemming from Marc's childhood. Despite Marc's seemingly final breakaway from Khonshu at the end of that series, he was once more co-opted by the god during Jason Aaron and Javier Garrón's *Age of Khonshu* event.[2] This arc saw Moon Knight face off against the Avengers on the moon god's behalf, before turning against him, again.

In Jed MacKay and Alessandro Cappuccio's Moon Knight run, Marc Spector has returned to the position of the high priest of Khonshu but is knowingly alienated from the god, despite still drawing on his power. This contradiction is the most representative of the character's history as a whole. Although Spector actively dislikes Khonshu's influence and what it forces him to do, he is consistently forced back into the god's service, almost as if he is addicted.

Moon Knight's internal conflict over his relationship with Khonshu is also representative of the conflict in many real-world religions. The tension between orthodox elements and those that want to adapt their belief systems. Lastly,

---

[1] *Moon Knight* Vol. 2, a.k.a. *Moon Knight: Fist of Khonshu*, which ran for 6 issues (March-Sept 1985).
[2] "Age of Khonshu." *The Avengers* Vol. 8 #33-37. By Jason Aaron and Javier Garrón.

although the version of Khonshu in the Marvel Universe has been fictionalized, a surprising amount of his characteristics originate from Ancient Egyptian beliefs and traditions, as represented by surviving archaeological evidence.

Marc Spector's belief in Khonshu stems from a single moment of moral clarity during his work as a mercenary. When his boss, Raoul Bushman, orders him to kill the daughter of an archaeologist, Marlene, Spector refuses, ultimately leading to his death in the tomb of Seti II. When the surviving villagers bring him to the tomb, he unexpectedly revives. Unlike most resurrections in Marvel Comics, it is unclear if this event involved any actual divine interference, or if Spector was ever really dead. Marc certainly thinks so, upon seeing the statue of Khonshu he declares himself, "a spectre of the moon... The moon's knight of vengeance,"[3] as thanks for being brought back to life, however, Marlene assumes that he is simply "delirious"[4] from his ordeal. Whatever the reason for Spector's recovery, his newfound faith in the moon god coincides with his moral awakening. This leads to the creation of Moon Knight as a force for good. Marlene reminds him of this when he confronts Bushman at the end of the first issue of *Moon Knight* Vol. 1, commenting that he needs to remember to "never abuse [his] power," and telling him, "You must never forget who [you] really [are.]"[5] The distinction between who Spector was as a mercenary, raised Jewish but pointedly not religious, and who he is as Moon Knight is very similar to religious stories featuring people who turn into a force of good in the world after finally seeing the light of a divine force. However, unlike most of those stories, Khonshu's divinity at this time is still actively in doubt.

Several issues later, in issue #5, Steven Grant asks Marc's best friend and fellow ex-mercenary, Frenchie, what he sees when he looks at the statue of Khonshu. During this period, the statue of Khonshu has been relocated to Grant's mansion, where it seems to act as Moon Knight's source of power. Grant acknowledges that it doesn't seem to make sense, but shares with Frenchie that he believes in the god's power, claiming it gives him "all kinds of weird vibrations... and when I stare at its face, I could swear I'm in contact with

---

[3] "The Macabre Moon Knight." *Moon Knight* Vol. 1 #1 (Nov 1980). By Doug Moench, Bill Sienkiewicz, and B. Sharen.

[4] Ibid.

[5] Ibid.

something inside it..."[6] Here, Moench includes the first reference to the possibility of Khonshu's existence outside of Spector's mental illness, with Frenchie admitting that the statue always gives him a "touch of [the] strange for me as well." Although this line of dialogue seems to imply that Khonshu's true nature as an actual god will be revealed soon, Moench takes Moon Knight's story in the opposite direction several issues later, when Bushman and another antagonist, Anton Mogart, known as The Midnight Man, team up.

Moon Knight Vol. 1 #9 opens with a promise on the cover page. "One minute ago, Moon Knight was destroyed. He doesn't know it yet."[7] Early in the story, Marlene and Samuels, Grant's butler, discuss Grant's supposed death in Egypt. Both express some level of disbelief in the supernatural aspect of the event but are unwilling to completely discount it. While Moon Knight is hunting down Bushman, who recently escaped from prison, the statue of Khonshu is stolen. Marlene elects not to tell Steven for fear of shaking his resolve. That is for nought when Moon Knight comes upon Mogart's hideout in the sewers and sees that he has the statue. Before the hero can respond, Mogart smashes the effigy, hoping that doing so will psychologically destabilize his foe. Mogart is revealed to be working with Bushman, who has set up the entire plan to get revenge on Spector for turning on him and defeating him.

In the second part of the story, in issue #10, Moon Knight escapes the trap. However, he is left in a haze, unsure of who he is or what he should be doing without Khonshu's presence in his life. Eventually, Marlene reveals another statue, one she claims to be the original. This is enough to bring the hero back to his senses and capture Bushman. Here, the very suggestion of Khonshu's realness is enough to restore Spector's facilities, which he acknowledges at the end of the issue. Khonshu's existence, Grant relays, no longer matters. If the god is real, then Marlene's restoration of the statue allowed Moon Knight to channel his power again. If not, then Spector had the power within him all along. This resolution seems to put the issue of Khonshu's realness to rest; Marc Spector has made peace with the fact that his god might not exist, and that possibility is no longer a direct threat to his mental stability.

---

[6] "Ghost Story." *Moon Knight* Vol. 1 #5 (1981). By Doug Moench, Bill Sienkiewicz, and Bob Sharen.
[7] "Vengeance in Reprise." *Moon Knight* Vol. 1 #9 (1981). By Doug Moench, Bill Sienkiewicz, and Bob Sharen.

Khonshu makes several additional appearances within the pages of *Moon Knight* Vol. 1 before Spector is forced to confront his faith once more. Two backup stories, featured in *Moon Knight* Vol. 1 #21 and #22, written by Alan Zelenetz and drawn by Greg LaRocque, showcase other people in the Marvel Universe who have faced the moon god's judgment. Although Khonshu is allegedly the main character of these stories, Zelenetz is careful not to disrupt the current status quo provided by the main stories; Khonshu's existence is still dubious. Both stories feature events that could be explained through Khonshu's divine power, such as trapping a thief in a sarcophagus[8] or turning the tide of a battle.[9] However, these events could also be explained as coincidence, with both stories leaving the characters and reader unsure of the truth. The same can be said of Steven and Marlene's next supposed encounter with Khonshu in *Moon Knight* Vol. 1 #28 when they are forced to revisit the tomb of Seti II by criminals posing as cultural researchers. Although doubt is reintroduced, a timely, single burst of wind allows Moon Knight to save both himself and Marlene; they conclude the adventure still sharing the belief that Khonshu most likely is not real, but theoretically could be.

Moon Knight Vol. 1 #28 is the last issue written by Doug Moench and drawn by Bill Sienkiewicz that directly engages with Khonshu as a potentially real figure. The implication that can be made is that Moench and Sienkiewicz intended to leave Khonshu's existence ambiguous. Importantly, at this point in the character's history, Moon Knight had made peace with the uncertainty of his faith, mirroring the struggle that people of faith often have in reality, due to the lack of any overt evidence of divine intervention. Had the stories of Marc Spector and Moon Knight ended when Moench and Sienkiewicz left the comic, that would have been a suitable final status quo for the character. *Moon Knight* would have been the story of a troubled man who used newfound faith to turn himself into a force for good in the world, and eventually realized that he only needed to have faith in himself. However, once Moench and Sienkiewicz left, Zelenetz became the primary writer for the series, and he had a very different idea of the role Khonshu should play in Moon Knight's narrative.

---

[8] "Tales of Khonshu: Murder by Moonlight." *Moon Knight* Vol. 1 #21 (1982). By Alan Zelenetz, Greg LaRocque, and Christie Scheele.
[9] "Tales of Khonshu: Moon over Alamein." *Moon Knight* Vol. 1 #22 (1982). By Alan Zelenetz, Greg LaRocque, and Christie Scheele.

When Zelenetz became the main writer for *Moon Knight* his goal was to reincorporate the supernatural aspects of the character that Moench had done away with.[10] This aim is obvious in the first issue of his tenure, *Moon Knight* Vol. 1 #36, which features Grant teaming up with Doctor Strange to save Marlene from an Ancient Egyptian spirit. At first, Grant is resistant to the idea that any supernatural forces exist, remembering his previous faith in Khonshu, and how Marlene brought him back to sanity. "You helped me see that I derived my strength from my own will and commitments, not from some long-dead mythology,"[11] Steven tells her, refusing to believe that Strange may be right about the incoming threat. This quote shows that Grant has drawn an explicit connection between his previous insanity and his belief in Khonshu; he later tells Strange that he won't return to his previous state of insane belief. Eventually, Moon Knight is forced to accept Strange's help, allowing him to engage in a mystic battle with the spirit. Grant is victorious, but the encounter leaves him unsettled. Now having proof of, at least some, supernatural forces being active in the world, he is forced to reexamine the possibility of his resurrection being mystical in nature. As Strange flies away to combat another threat, Grant admits to Marlene that he believes the doctor, saying, "I don't for one minute like the idea... but I believe him."[12] This statement represents another shift in Moon Knight's perspective on Khonshu; while he has operated in a state of either disbelief or the belief that Khonshu's status does not matter. Grant is now forced to realize that it is extremely likely that Khonshu is real. This realization leads to disastrous consequences.

After the original *Moon Knight* series was cancelled, Marvel released a short-lived second volume. This second series was titled *Fist of Khonshu: Moon Knight.* It was written by Zelenetz, and penciled by Chris Warner, and features Grant and Marlene enjoying a life of luxury now that Steven has fully retired from the Moon Knight persona. However, when the statue of Khonshu is bought by the Avatar of Anubis, Grant receives a summons to return to action. Although Marlene threatens to leave him if he does, Grant boards a plane to

---

[10] *Marvel Moon Knight Epic Collection: Final Rest* (2018). By Robert J. Sodaro. Page 486.
[11] "Ghosts." *Moon Knight* Vol. 1 #36 (1984). By Alan Zelenetz, Bo Hampton, and Ben Shaw.
[12] Ibid.

Egypt, claiming that "this time, I have to go with the voices in my head."[13] There he encounters members of a cult dedicated to Khonshu who give him new weapons and information. Finally, Moon Knight has confirmation that Khonshu is real. Marlene would remain skeptical until witnessing Marc being resurrected again through Khonshu's will, during the miniseries *Moon Knight: Resurrection Wars*.[14]

Now that the issue of Khonshu's existence had been put to rest, with Spector and his supporting cast acknowledging that the moon god was real, writers were able to tell new stories specifically about the relationship between Spector and Khonshu.

In 2006, Charlie Huston and David Finch launched a new Moon Knight series. The first issue of which opens with a broken Spector reminiscing about his days as a hero, begging Khonshu to help him once more. Marc, Steven, and Jake previously only had to deal with the paradoxical nature of belief in terms of their relationship with Khonshu, they are now forced to accept that Khonshu is real, but they no longer wish to have fealty to him.

Within Huston's *Moon Knight* stories, Khonshu is given characteristics that greatly differ from what one would expect from a divine figure. He is mean, and sarcastic, often finding delight in torturing Spector, appearing in the form of Bushman, whom Marc killed after cutting off his face. Despite Spector's aversion to this new form, he still prays to Khonshu, desperate to recover from his injuries and regain control of his life.

While Marc regains the use of his legs, allowing him to operate as Moon Knight again, Huston's first story arc, *The Bottom*,[15] ends with a crushing revelation. Khonshu was responsible for Moon Knight and Bushman's final confrontation, having orchestrated the entire series of events to make Marc a more compliant and willing avatar. This betrayal sets the stage for a new status quo between Marc Spector and Khonshu, one that is still largely in place in the present day. To Marc, Khonshu is an addiction; something that he wishes he could break free of but is always pulled back to.

---

[13] "Night of the Jackal." *Moon Knight* Vol. 2 #1 (1985). By Alan Zelenetz, Chris Warner, and Christie Scheele.

[14] *Moon Knight: Resurrection War* #1-4 (Nov 1997 to Feb 1998). By Doug Moench and Tommy Lee Edwards.

[15] "The Bottom." *Moon Knight* Vol. 5 #1-6 (2006). By Charlie Huston, David Finch, and Frank D'Armata.

Huston's *Moon Knight* Vol. 5, which is later continued by Mike Benson, features Marc Spector trying to pull himself out of Khonshu's grasp. First, Khonshu forces him to register with S.H.I.E.L.D. so that his acts of vengeance can continue, arguing that "this way you get what you need to do. [And I] get the exposure I require." When Spector agrees, Khonshu is unsurprised, saying, "Of course you will. Was there ever any doubt?"[16] showing the unwilling influence the god has over him. Later, Marc is trying to show restraint when dealing with criminals, which Khonshu finds laughable, constantly encouraging him to maim or kill them.

Throughout this volume, Marc is at odds with Khonshu, a far cry from both his original devout belief in the god and his uneasy acceptance of the god's potential nonexistence. More importantly, Marc giving in to Khonshu consistently leads to tragedy within these stories. Khonshu's bloodlust led Marc to cut off Bushman's face, which in turn led to Spector's life falling apart. While hunting down his old enemy, Carson Knowles, the Black Spectre, Moon Knight finally gives in to Khonshu's demands for violence. He pushes Knowles off a roof, killing him to prevent him from taking control of countless civilians. Although Khonshu is rejoiceful, telling Spector, "You're a star again, kid!"[17] Every other character present, including Marc himself, reacts with shock and disgust. Afterwards, Marc attempts to cut all ties with the entity, forcefully saying he is "done."[18] This is represented in the run by the ever-present statue of Khonshu being smashed.

Khonshu is largely absent from the next story arc, leaving Marc alone to deal with the consequences of his actions, and being hunted by the Thunderbolts.[19] The eventual outcome is the temporary death of the Marc Spector persona, leaving Jake Lockley as the primary personality. Quickly Khonshu starts appearing to Jake, urging him to return to killing. The fact that Khonshu still engages with Lockley, despite Spector's disavowal of him, shows

---

[16] "The Uses of Restraint." *Moon Knight* Vol. 5 #13 (2007). By Charlie Huston, Tomm Coker, and Dean White.

[17] "God and Country: Conclusion." *Moon Knight* Vol 5 #19 (2008). By Mike Benson, Mark Texeira, and Dan Brown.

[18] Ibid.

[19] "The Death of Marc Spector." *Moon Knight* Vol. 5 #21-25 (2008-2009). By Mike Benson, Mark Texeira, Javier Saltares, and Dan Brown.

that their codependency works both ways. Despite his insistence to the contrary, Khonshu needs Moon Knight just as much as Moon Knight needs him.

Much like the wax and waning of the moon, Khonshu's overt power over Spector, Lockley, and Grant also shifts. In the next series, *Vengeance of the Moon Knight*, by Greg Hurwitz and various artists, Khonshu has significantly less influence over Lockley's actions. He is as petulant and demanding as he was in Huston and Benson's series, but Khonshu's new role as the less powerful one in the relationship is represented by his depiction as being physically smaller. Notably, Lockley is much more successful than Spector at rehabilitating Moon Knight's image as a hero. Specifically going out of his way to avoid seriously maiming criminals and even reconciling with Frenchie and Marlene, who were at odds with Marc for much of the previous volume.

Throughout the series, however, Khonshu grows larger and larger, demonstrating his power is beginning to wax once again. When Lockley is brought face to face with a resurrected Bushman, Khonshu is at his zenith, depicted in a splash page as towering over the burning factory right next to the fight, demanding that Moon Knight obey him and return Bushman to the grave. Unlike the last time, however, Jake denies Khonshu, allowing him to move past the god's demands and become an actual superhero, even rejoining a faction of the Avengers.

Of course, given the nature of comics, Khonshu quickly regains himself and reappears during the *Shadowland* three-issue tie-in miniseries. The series ends with Moon Knight killing his brother, (*again*) and Marc Spector making a reappearance on the final page. Khonshu's return once again highlights the addiction relationship, Marc's high comes from his belief and acts of violence.

In 2016, Jeff Lemire and Greg Smallwood further defined Spector and Khonshu's relationship. This volume opens with Marc trapped in an asylum and no memory of the circumstances that led him to that place. All the members of his supporting cast, including Frenchie and Marlene, are patients there too, and he learns from Khonshu that the Egyptian gods, Seth in particular, have invaded the physical world. Once they escape the asylum, however, Marc discovers the truth, that Khonshu designed the entire environment as a trap to convince Marc to let the god take his physical form. Lemire reveals that Khonshu and Marc's relationship did not start when Marc was dying in the tomb, but rather that Khonshu has been grooming Marc to be his avatar since he was a child.

Here, Khonshu takes on characteristics found more commonly in Judeo-Christian beliefs than that of the Ancient Egyptians, referring to himself as

Spector's "father."[20] Khonshu continues doing so even after Marc realizes the trap and decides to end the god once and for all. This is Khonshu at his most powerful, preparing to fully possess Spector and kill his mind. Spector is only able to defeat Khonshu by reconciling with all of his alters, declaring that they "are Moon Knight. And we never needed you,"[21][22] as they smash Khonshu's skull. In this moment Marc fully reclaims his power from Khonshu, maybe for the first time since the god's existence was confirmed. If this had been the last Moon Knight story ever told, the character's history would end with the priest finally vanquishing his insolent god. Of course, this being comics, the story continued, but the *Marvel Legacy Moon Knight* series, written by Max Bemis and drawn by several artists, that followed depicted Khonshu as only having the same amount of influence as any of Spector's alters, showing that after his defeat, his power has significantly waned.

The next time Khonshu plays a large role in Marc Spector's life is several years later, during Jason Aaron and Javier Garrón's *Avengers* storyline, *The Age of Khonshu*.[23] Once again, Khonshu has regained his power and uses Marc to attack the Avengers, believing that he is the only one who can save the world from Mephisto. Spector does so, but the difference this time is that he is fully aware of the cycle, thanks to his experiences during Huston, Benson, Hurwitz, and Lemire's series. Unlike the early issues written by Huston, Spector does not beg Khonshu for power, instead, he takes it while actively planning to betray Khonshu once the god's time has run out. Eventually, he does so, with a timely assist from the Phoenix Force, but the event leaves Spector on the outs with everyone, including his friends and family, the Avengers, and of course, the god he betrayed.

The current Moon Knight volume, Vol. 10, written by Jed MacKay and drawn primarily by Alessandro Cappuccio, opens with a relatively simple concept. Spector, now thinking of himself as an apostate or heretical priest (thanks to his betrayal of Khonshu), has opened a Midnight Mission to provide

---

[20] "Birth and Death, Part One." *Moon Knight* Vol. 8 #10 (2017). By Jeff Lemire, Greg Smallwood, and Jordie Bellaire.

[21]

[22] "Birth and Death, Part Five." *Moon Knight* Vol. 8 #14 (2017). By Jeff Lemire, Greg Smallwood, and Jordie Bellaire.

[23] "Age of Khonshu." *The Avengers* Vol. 8 #33-37 (2020). By Jason Aaron and Javier Garron.

aid and protection to "those who travel at night."[24] He is directly aware of the contradiction; when asked by his therapist about his current relationship with Khonshu, he replies, "I know Khonshu is unworthy of my worship [...] but unworthy or not, I am his fist,"[25] showing that despite his issues with the god, Spector still believes he is indebted to him. Paradoxically, this Moon Knight is the most removed from Khonshu since his early history, but the most observant in his duties as the fist of Khonshu. This paradox is made explicit through Marc's early conflicts with Dr. Badr, who, unlike Spector, is a loyal fist of Khonshu known as Hunter's Moon. The conflict between Spector and Badr is representative of the conflict between real-world religious orthodoxy and more liberal religious factions.

When they first encounter each other, in issue #1 of Vol 10, Marc has expanded his definition of "those who travel at night"[26] to include a group of forcibly turned vampires. According to those same beliefs, Badr believes they should be executed. The two eventually form an uneasy alliance, agreeing that they serve the same god although they have different opinions of him, showing that compromise between two sects is possible. MacKay's run seems primed to continue exploring the relationship between Marc and Khonshu, as the latest issue at the time of this writing, has Moon Knight contact the god for help for the first time since the Age of Khonshu ended.[27] To what end that relationship will extend is unclear, but Khonshu's influence over his knight has been on the wane and might be starting to wax once more.

Despite Khonshu's absence from MacKay's series so far, the author has done much to develop Spector's relationship with the moon god. Rather than simply being a devout or lapsed follower, MacKay has Spector explicitly express his feelings towards Khonshu, specifically, that the relationship between them makes Marc feel like a failure. He compares himself unfavourably to his father, a rabbi, saying "*I* was the weak one. I sold out everything I had been raised to believe in to save my own neck [...] My father's god took us out of Egypt. My

---

[24] "The Midnight Mission: Part One." *Moon Knight* Vol. 10 #1 (2021). By Jed MacKay, Alessandro Cappuccio, and Rachelle Rosenberg.
[25] Ibid.
[26] Ibid.
[27] "The Killing Time, Part One." *Moon Knight* Vol. 10 #11 (2022). By Jed MacKay, Alessandro Cappuccio, and Rachelle Rosenberg.

Page 13 of *Moon Knight* Vol. 10 #11.

new god had kept us there."[28] This confession shows Spector finally confronting a new aspect of the trauma of his death and resurrection, helping explain his antagonistic relationship with Khonshu. The moon god saved his life but is also a constant reminder of everything that Marc hates about himself Further showing why they have been perpetually estranged since Spector learned that he was real. An abstract idea is easy to put faith in. An actual being, who has proven time and time again how fallible they are, is much harder.

Marc Spector's relationship with Khonshu is interesting to study throughout his history as a character, however, it is also fascinating to observe how Spector's observed worship correlates to the mythology of Khonshu in Ancient Egypt. As is claimed several times throughout Moon Knight's history, Khonshu, or Khonsu due to alternate spellings, was known during the New Kingdom period, from the 16th century to the 12th century BCE, as "the Greatest of the Great Gods."[29] According to ancient texts, Khonsu would travel across the night sky in a boat, similar to Ra's journey during the day as the sun. The name Khonsu means "the traveller," which explains the association Moench drew between Khonsu and the need to protect travellers of the night in the original Moon Knight series.

Khonshu's tendencies toward violence in Marvel Comics also originate from ancient texts; early sources known as the Pyramid Texts and the Coffin Texts, from the Old and Middle Kingdoms respectively, refer to Khonshu as "Khonsu, who slew the lords, who strangle them for the King," and being "capable of sending out 'the rage which burns hearts.'"[30] This *rage* is on full display during Huston and Benson's Moon Knight series, giving Khonshu's depiction as a sadistic force historical credence. Surprisingly, however, Khonsu was most well-known during his time of prominence as a healing god, with knowledge of his restorative power spread beyond Egypt.[31] This fact directly contradicts how Khonshu is depicted within the Marvel Universe, considering he is often responsible for the deterioration of Spector's mental health. However, it does

---

[28] "The Midnight Mission, Part Five." *Moon Knight* Vol. 10 #5 (2022). By Jed MacKay, Alessandro Cappuccio, and Rachelle Rosenberg.
[29] Redford, Donald B. (ed.). *The Oxford Essential Guide to Egyptian Mythology.* Oxford University Press, 2003. Page 186.
[30] Ibid.
[31] Ibid, page 187.

help explain the clemency Spector recently offered a group of vampires. He is trying to channel a new facet of Khonshu's power.

Elements from early Moon Knight comics bear a striking resemblance to a text that details Khonsu's role as a healer during the New Kingdom period, the Bentresh Stela. The Bentresh Stela was found in a Ptolemaic chapel that was originally near a temple for Khonsu in Karnak.[32] The stela details how the Prince of Bakhtan's younger daughter fell ill due to a "ghost."[33] The Prince asks Rameses II to send a god to drive out the spirit, causing Rameses to consult Khonsu in his aspect of "Khonsu in Thebes Neferhotep."[34] The god appears to agree to provide his service, and the Prince is sent a statue of *Khonsu the Authority*, to dispel the illness.[35] Khonsu does so, but then the Prince refuses to return the statue to Thebes until Khonsu sends him a vision demanding he does so.[36]

Khonsu's power in the Bentresh Stela is tied specifically to the statue representing him, much like how Moon Knight's power and belief in the deity only existed when he had ownership of the statue of Khonshu in early issues of *Moon Knight*.[37] Ultimately, Marvel Comics adapted the figure of Khonshu to serve their storytelling purpose, however, it is surprising how many elements of Khonshu and Moon Knight's personalities and characteristics can be traced back to Ancient Egypt's view of the god.

Over the course of Moon Knight's multi-decade publication history, the god Khonshu has held many different positions. At first, Khonshu was simply a delusion, something Marc Spector believed in, but everyone else thought was a result of his near-death trauma. Then Khonshu became something more akin to a fairy tale, something that even Marc didn't believe in, although there was still room within the story for the god's existence to be proven true. When Khonshu was proven to exist, first by Doctor Strange's real magic and later by a cult

---

[32] Simpson, William Kelly (ed.). *The Literature of Ancient Egypt: an Anthology of Stories, Instructions, and Poetry*. Translated by Robert Kriech Ritner, William Kelly Simpson, Vincent A. Tobin, and Edward F. Wente Jr. Yale University Press, 2003. Page 361.

[33] Ibid, page 364.

[34] Ibid. page 364.

[35] Ibid, page 364-365.

[36] Ibid, page 365-366.

[37] Most notably in *Moon Knight* Vol. 1 #9-10 (1981). By Doug Moench, Bill Sienkiewicz, and Bob Sharen.

group that helped Moon Knight return to action, the relationship between him and Spector shifted, turning toxic. The aspect of Khonshu that Spector dealt with became increasingly obsessed with violence, while Marc attempted to regain control from the god who irrevocably altered his life. Later, that conflict lost all sub-textuality, becoming an explicit battle between the two for Spector's very body.

The nature of American comics meant that Khonshu couldn't be permanently removed from Moon Knight's supporting cast, so his next appearance featured him as simply an additional alter within Spector's system. *The Age of Khonshu* placed the god back in power, but Spector, now aware of the cycle the two are trapped in, prepared to betray him, leaving him on the wane once again. A study of texts from Ancient Egypt also reveals that a surprising amount of Khonshu's characteristics within the Marvel Universe have origins within real-world myths.

Currently, Spector is operating as an apostate priest. Despite the internal contradiction of that title, and the knowledge that his god is "not worthy of worship,"[38] Marc Spector is committed to being Khonshu's fist in a different way, and although some might tell him he is doing his job poorly, the truth is that their opinions do not matter. By showing Moon Knight adapting his religious beliefs to better serve his neighbourhood and the modern world, MacKay offers an allegory for how religious beliefs in the real world can adapt to modern times. Some might argue that a character as historically violent as Moon Knight, thanks largely to Khonshu's influence, should not be featured in publications today, however, they miss the entire point of the character. Moon Knight is not a character of violence, but one of change, going through different phases, much like the moon that he and his god represent.

---

[38] "The Midnight Mission, Part One." *Moon Knight* Vol. 10 #1 (2021). By Jed MacKay, Alessandro Cappuccio, Rachelle Rosenberg.

We are Moon Knight

by Leyna Vincent of the Douglas J. Vincent System

Dissociative identity disorder (abbreviated to DID, formerly known as Multiple Personality Disorder or MPD) is one of the most misunderstood and unfairly maligned mental health diagnoses. As an alter in a DID system myself, I know this all too well, and it has affected my life in ways that go far beyond merely being offended by an inaccurate portrayal in a movie or television show.

The depictions of DID in fiction, even when combined with fantastical elements like superpowers or futuristic technology, may still influence how the actual disorder is viewed by the general public. Most of whom know very little accurate information about DID. As a result, when DID is depicted inaccurately, or in an overly negative light in fiction, it can adversely affect how those of us who have DID are treated. Unfortunately, the vast majority of fictional depictions of DID have been highly inaccurate and filled with stigmatizing stereotypes. This is even frequently true of fact-based portrayals, which are often exaggerated for dramatic effect. As a member of a system, I am going to explore some of the frequent factual inaccuracies and some of the common negative, stigmatizing tropes. I will then relate this to how *Moon Knight* comic books fare in the accuracy and positivity of their portrayal of this disorder.

One of the most common inaccuracies, as portrayed in media, is that DID systems are always overt. In other words, it is easy for outsiders to spot noticeable differences between alters. In many movies and TV shows featuring DID, each alter will have their own outfit that they wear whenever they are out and their own distinct accent or manner of speaking. A good example of this is in the 2009-2011 Showtime television series *The United States of Tara*, in which each of Tara's alters had a different mode of dress and speech. This was even highlighted on the promotional posters and DVD/Blu-ray covers for the series. While this is an easy way to convey switching to the audience, it's not nearly as common as fiction would have you believe. This is because the nature of DID is built for hiding. The purpose of diverging separate identities is to help separate the intense feelings caused by traumatic experiences so that the person can appear to be more emotionally stable and *normal.*

Dr Richard P. Kluft, one of the co-founders of the *International Society for the Study of Trauma and Dissociation*, discussed in an interview with the *System Speak podcast* how learning about this hidden nature of DID helped him diagnose it during his early days treating dissociative patients. Dr Kluft states:

> If you learn the hidden characteristics of something, and that the usual idea of what a DID patient looks like is incorrect – like, come on, it's not a flying circus, it's not a Mouseketeers roll call, with everyone jumping out and saying "I'm Joe, I'm Jill, I'm this, I'm that" – it's a psychopathology of hiddenness. So, by looking at it with subtle questions, I found I had a nice screening measure, and was finding cases right and left.[1]

Therefore, this misconception of DID being extremely overt can contribute to it being misdiagnosed. I believe this may be part of why our system was misdiagnosed for nine years before we finally received the correct diagnosis.

As for the portrayal of this misconception in *Moon Knight*, there are different outfits that the alters in Marc's system wear. However, I suggest this is related to their roles more than to who they are as an alter. For instance, Jake Lockley wears shabby street clothes and a fake moustache to fit in with his street-level informants without being recognized as Marc Spector. Meanwhile, Steven Grant wears expensive suits to fit in with his high society contacts. Jake talks more casually, using street lingo, and Steven speaks in a more refined way. Overall, the switches are usually fairly subtle, to the point that Marlene, who lives with Marc and knows about all of the alters, sometimes has difficulty telling who is out in the body at any given time.

Another one of the most common factual errors about DID in media is thinking that it's the same as schizophrenia. These are two separate disorders,

---

[1] Sunshaw, Emma, and Richard P. Kluft. "Dissociative Identity Disorder (Multiple Personality Disorder), Complex Trauma, and Dissociation." *System Speak*, 2021. www.systemspeak.org

which are in different categories of disorder in the Diagnostic and Statistical Manual of Mental Disorders (DSM).[2] Schizophrenia is classified as a psychotic disorder, whereas DID is classified as a dissociative disorder. So why are people with clear-cut dissociative identities referred to as schizophrenic so often in fiction? There are a variety of reasons. First, the Latin roots for the word schizophrenia translate to *split mind*. This understandably makes people think of DID, but it refers to either the mind's split from reality or the split between rational and emotional thinking processes, rather than a split of a person's identity. People with schizophrenia often experience visual and auditory hallucinations, which can include seeing people or hearing voices that aren't their own. This also causes confusion with DID since people with DID can often see and hear the other alters/identities within their minds, which can be mistaken for hallucinations. Also, many stories about DID portray the person as seeing hallucinations of the other alters outside of their own body. While this can happen with DID, it's not nearly as common as it is with schizophrenia. We usually *see* the other alters only in our mind's eye, not in the external world.

In *Moon Knight*, the term schizophrenia, or the derogatory abbreviation *schizo*, was used fairly often to refer to Marc Spector in the seventies and eighties. In more recent years, the writers of *Moon Knight* usually use the appropriate term of Dissociative Identity Disorder but still sometimes use tropes that can lead to confusion, such as the hallucination of alters in the external world. One example of this is #10 of the Jeff Lemire run,[3] which shows a flashback to Marc's childhood. Marc saw the alter Steven Grant as a separate boy in the external world, but Marc's father did not see Steven.

Of the common problems with positivity in media portrayals of DID, probably the most prevalent (and also the most stigmatizing) is the trope of at least one alter in the DID system being extremely violent and sadistic. Acting as a personification of all of the evil in the system's mind. However, research on DID clarifies that the perpetration of violent crimes by DID systems is nowhere near as common as portrayed in fiction.

---

[2] DSM version 5 was published in 2013 and is the most up-to-date version at the time of writing this essay.

[3] "Birth and Death, Part One." *Moon Knight* Vol. 8 #10 (2017). By Jeff Lemire, Greg Smallwood, and Jordie Bellaire.

In a 2017 study, Dr Aliya R. Webermann and Dr Bethany L. Brand questioned a sample of 173 dissociative disorder patients about their involvement with the criminal justice system over the past six months. It was found that "3% had a legal charge, 1.8% received a fine(s), 1.2% received a criminal justice mental health referral, and only 0.6% had been incarcerated. None of the DID patients reported convictions or probation during the past 6 months."[4] Despite these low percentages, the stereotype of the violent/evil alter persists and is perpetuated by movies such as *Psycho, Identity, Fight Club, Split,* and *Glass,* to name just a few. This stereotype can most likely be traced back to the 1886 novel by Robert Louis Stevenson, *The Strange Case of Dr Jekyll and Mr Hyde.* This novel, however, was not about DID, but rather about a scientist experimenting on himself to separate the good and evil sides of his nature.

For the most part, *Moon Knight* comics have managed to avoid specifically labelling any of Marc's alters as evil. They have portrayed him as having an extremely violent past in the CIA and as a mercenary. Although this violence wasn't specifically tied to his DID or his alters. However, there have been some *Moon Knight* stories that have claimed that one alter is more violent than the others. This was often specified as Marc in the early *Moon Knight* stories. In more recent stories, Jake Lockley is the more violent one. For example, in the second issue of Max Bemis's *Moon Knight* run,[5] Marc purposely lets Jake out, because he is the only one vicious enough to deal with the villain known as The Truth. Moon Knight's violent behaviour has frequently been portrayed as more severe than most other Marvel superheroes, with a few notable exceptions, such as Wolverine, the Punisher, and Deadpool.

In addition to the *evil alter* trope, another negative portrayed in media is the excessive focus on sufferers being perpetually weak, crazy, and unable to live fulfilling lives. We are often shown as being a constant burden to our friends and family, or worse, as having no friends or family to speak of because we have scared or driven them away. We are shown as being unable to

---

[4] Webermann, Aliya R. and Bethany L. Brand. "Mental Illness and Violent Behavior: the Role of Dissociation." *Borderline Personality Disorder and Emotion Dysregulation* Vol. 4, article #2, 2017.

[5] "Crazy Runs in The Family, Part Two." *Moon Knight* Vol. 9 #2 (2018). By Max Bemis, Jacen Burrows, and Mat Lopes. Note: the same issue is numbered #189 in its so-called "legacy numbering."

overcome substance abuse, keep a job, find love, and live on our own for any length of time without being in and out of mental institutions. To be honest, living with DID is extremely difficult, and all these things can, and do, apply to some DID systems. We have been admitted to a behavioural health facility due to an addiction to self-harm, and we have lost friends due to our erratic behaviour. However, these struggles are made worse when media depictions of DID systems gratuitously focus on the worst aspects of the disorder. Painting a bleak, hopeless picture for anyone newly diagnosed with DID. They fail to show any hope that a DID system can overcome their struggles and learn to live a happy, fulfilled life. Our system has found that, through a lot of therapy and hard work, overcoming our trauma, it is possible to become more stable and functional in our shared life. Some DID systems choose to pursue integration, a merging of the alters, but that doesn't work for everyone. It certainly didn't work for us, but we have found that by working together to cooperate and have mutual respect, we can learn to function well as an internal family, sharing our lives and helping each other to achieve our goals.

Over the years, *Moon Knight* comics have been hit and miss when it comes to this sort of overly hopeless portrayal of DID. There have been times creators have shown Marc Spector as being extremely weak and alone, most notably in the arc "The Bottom," written by Charlie Huston.[6] However, in most instances, including that one, it was followed by arcs showing Marc working to get his act together and pull himself/themselves out of the slump. There are several arcs, such as the issues following the "Scarlet Redemption" arc in *Marc Spector: Moon Knight*[7] and the *Vengeance of the Moon Knight* series, which depict the Moon Knight system showing genuine remorse for their past, and trying to be a less violent, more noble superhero. Unfortunately, regardless of how many times this happens, when he interacts with other heroes in the Marvel universe, they usually see him as *the crazy one* and tend to be cautious of trusting him.

These are not nearly all the ways DID is inaccurately or negatively portrayed in media, but they are some of the most common and potentially damaging. Having given an overview, I will now explore in more depth, how various

---

[6] "The Bottom." *Moon Knight* Vol. 5 #1-6 (2006). By Charlie Huston, David Finch, and Frank D'Armata.
[7] Issues #32-33 of *Marc Spector: Moon Knight*, which followed the "Scarlet Redemption" arc (issues #26-31).

volumes and specific arcs of *Moon Knight* have fared over the years, in both the accuracy and positivity of their portrayal of DID.

Moon Knight had a secret identity, Marc Spector, from his first appearance in *Werewolf by Night* #32 in 1975. His additional identities of millionaire Steven Grant and cab driver Jake Lockley first appeared in *Marvel Spotlight* #28, the following year. Doug Moench, co-creator and original writer of Moon Knight continued to explore these identities in several appearances of the character in *Hulk* magazine and *Marvel Preview* in 1978, before bringing them into Moon Knight's first solo title in 1980. From these early appearances, it appears that Moench intended Grant and Lockley to be aliases that Marc uses to further his crime-fighting career as Moon Knight. Moench himself has confirmed this in an interview with the *Into the Knight* podcast, in which he said, "It all, to me, was a logical progression. And, you know, Marc Spector is the real guy, but the real guy has decided to change, right? ... And Lockley is phoney, and Steven Grant is phoney... He meets Marlene as Steven Grant, and she's kinda in love with that part of him ... so Steven Grant starts to become more of the dominant one."[8] As far as Moench was concerned the other identities were created as a conscious decision by Marc, followed by the conscious decision to make Grant more prominent due to Marlene's preference for that identity.

However, it didn't take long before Moench started to muddy the waters by dropping hints that Marc's aliases might be starting to develop into serious mental health issues. Of course, as with many portrayals of DID from the 1980s, Moench misidentified it as schizophrenia almost every time it was mentioned. For instance, in *Marvel Spotlight* #29, Marc tells his helicopter pilot Frenchie, "Y'see, I've gotta flirt with schizophrenia again-- / --and make a quick-change to Lockley now..."[9] In this case, it seems like Marc is joking, but in later issues, his girlfriend Marlene starts to express concern about his mental health. In the Moon Knight story "The Big Blackmail" from *Hulk!* Magazine #13, as Steven Grant changes into his cabbie outfit and gets ready to leave as Jake Lockley, Marlene tells him, "Hmp—just like that—a change of brain with a change of clothes. / I suggest you read "Sybil", Steven—or Jake. / You're playing with fire,

---

[8] "Episode 100: Loony-Palooza." Into the Knight: The Moon Knight Modcast, 2019. By Rey Gesmundo.
[9] "The Deadly Gambit of Conquer-Lord!" *Marvel Spotlight* Vol. 1 #29 (1976). By Doug Moench, Don Perlin, and Irene Vartanoff.

you know."[10] Here Marlene is referring to the book *Sybil* by Flora Schreiber, about the real-life case of Sybil Dorsett, who was diagnosed with dissociative identity disorder (or multiple personality disorder, as it was known at the time). The implication being that Marc, by changing between identities so often, is risking developing DID. Then, in issue #2 of the first ongoing *Moon Knight* series, Steven Grant admits that there is an emotional difference between Moon Knight and the other three identities. He tells Marlene, "Me, Lockley, and even Marc Spector are too normal. Capable of too much emotion...including fear. / Moon Knight is pure—a primal force stripped of emotion; a being who can get the job done without conflicting feelings." Marlene responds by saying, "That's bull, Steven, and you know it. And it scares me." To which Steven replies, "Moon Knight scares you." Marlene tells him, "Even so. Even if there is a big difference, it's all in your mind. I wish you'd admit it before you get yourself killed."[11] So, again, Marlene is concerned that his identity changes are affecting his mental health, and it could even result in his death if he continues as Moon Knight. There are several more instances of Marlene raising these types of concerns in subsequent issues of the first volume of *Moon Knight*, but the gist is that Marlene is afraid that even though these identities started as aliases, they could develop into an actual mental illness.

Marlene didn't need to worry, however, because all the top researchers in the field of dissociation agree that DID is caused by childhood trauma and cannot be created on purpose through fantasy. DID skeptics have tried to debunk this by claiming that DID can be created iatrogenically (through suggestion), either from a therapist or exposure to media about DID. In a paper about common DID myths written by several top dissociation researchers including Dr Bethany Brand, the authors dispute there is evidence for this theory. They write, "Despite the concerns of fantasy model theorists that DID is iatrogenically created, *no study in any clinical population supports the fantasy model of dissociation*."[12] Therefore, if Marc's other identities truly were aliases

---

[10] "The Big Blackmail." *Hulk! Magazine* Vol. 1 #13 (1979). By Doug Moench, Bill Sienkiewicz, and Steven Oliff.
[11] "The Slasher." *Moon Knight* Vol. 1 #2 (1980). By Doug Moench, Bill Sienkiewicz, and Bob Sharen.
[12] Brand, Bethany L., Vedat Sar, Pam Stavropoulos, Christa Krüger, Marilyn Korzekwa, Alfonso Martínez-Taboas, and Warwick Middleton. "Separating Fact

that he created from his imagination, it would not be possible for them to develop into DID.

In later years, writers of *Moon Knight*, such as Jeff Lemire and Max Bemis, have retroactively introduced that Marc has DID by canonising his other identities as existing since childhood, created due to traumatic events. If this is the case, then that would mean Steven, Jake, and even Moon Knight were alters, and Marc was only fooling himself by thinking that they were aliases he created on purpose. Speaking from personal experience, as well as that of other DID systems we have met, this is not all that far-fetched. DID often goes undiagnosed or misdiagnosed until well into adulthood, and until we receive that diagnosis, we often try to minimize any awareness we have of our alters by thinking they are delusions or imaginary friends, or other similar rationalizations. Therefore, it wouldn't be beyond the realm of possibility, even if Moench originally intended otherwise, that Marc Spector's aliases could be dissociative identities.

Possibly the most powerful evidence for the case of Marc having DID in any of Doug Moench's stories is in *Moon Knight* #7. It's a very small panel, but it speaks volumes. It comes right after Jake Lockley has been talking on the phone with Marlene. She persists in calling him Steven, even after he tells her that he's Jake now. Jake asks her to a book hotel room for Steven Grant and herself, and one each for Frenchie and Crawley, at the Drake Hotel in Chicago, and Grant will be home after Jake finishes eating at Gena's. After he gets off the phone with Marlene, in a small panel, Jake thinks to himself, "The lady's a gem. / Grant don't deserve her."[13] It's obvious from this panel that Jake is jealous that Marlene is in love with Steven. Before this, when the various identities talked about each other to Marlene, they played it off as a joke. In this instance, however, since Jake is thinking silently, there is no reason for him to joke about it. Also, if all the identities were Marc Spector, there would be no reason for him to feel jealous of himself. Again, speaking from personal experience, I know that jealousy among alters in a DID system can and does happen since we think of each other as separate identities. So, it can be demonstrated, that Marc's

---

from Fiction: An Empirical Examination of Six Myths About Dissociative Identity Disorder." *Harvard Review of Psychiatry* Vol. 24 #4 (2016).

[13] "The Moon Kings." *Moon Knight* Vol. 1 #7 (1980). By Doug Moench, Bill Sienkiewicz, and Don Warfield.

aliases were actually alters in a DID system by this point in the character's history, even though Moench claimed that this wasn't his original intention.

Assuming, then, that these alters had existed since Marc's childhood, and they were only deluding themselves that they were intentionally created aliases, we can highlight these early Doug Moench Moon Knight stories as a fairly positive portrayal of DID. Although, they were far from being factually accurate. As stated previously, they quite often referred to Marc's mental condition as schizophrenia, even though his symptoms were far closer to DID. Also, Moench seemed to imply that intentionally created aliases could evolve into alters over time, which is not how DID works. The reason I claim these stories were a positive representation of DID despite being highly inaccurate, is because the Moon Knight system seemed to be a highly functional one. It seems clear the alters in the system had a high level of co-consciousness, meaning they were aware of each other and had a common awareness of what was going on in their collective life in the external world. They aren't shown to have amnesia of events that happened when a different alter was out. Although it is very common for DID systems to have amnesia, and in fact, it's one of the criteria for a diagnosis of DID. The amount of amnesia is something that can be reduced over time, through therapy and learning ways of increasing co-consciousness between alters. So, in this way, the Moon Knight system is functioning healthily, like a system that has made a lot of progress through years of therapy.

Another way in which the Moon Knight system appears to be highly functioning in these early stories is their level of cooperation with each other. They seem to be very aware of, and comfortable with, their roles within the system, and how those roles interplay to achieve their collective goal of fighting crime. Steven Grant is the refined, sophisticated one, who maintains their finances and their contacts in high society circles. Jake Lockley is the much more casual, low-brow alter who obtains information from street-level informants. Marc Spector is the one that they try to keep locked away, for fear of his callous violence, but the knowledge and contacts he acquired in his mercenary days are still useful at times. Moon Knight is the ultimate expression of their crime-fighting mission. They can switch seamlessly and rapidly from one alter to the next, according to which one is best suited for the task at hand. Again, this is something that doesn't come easy to DID systems. Switching on purpose is something that can only happen with the cooperation of both alters involved in the switch. If one of them doesn't want to switch, it will be extremely difficult, in fact near impossible, for the other to force it to happen. The level of cooperation and highly defined roles that the Moon Knight system exhibits is also usually only achieved in a DID system after years of therapy and a lot of hard work. Therefore, in both co-consciousness and cooperation, these Doug Moench stories show a DID system that, in many ways, has accomplished what many systems work very hard to achieve. In this way, these stories represent a very positive and hopeful portrayal of DID.

Following the first *Moon Knight* series there was a 6-issue run, *Fist of Khonshu: Moon Knight,* and a 60-issue run called *Marc Spector: Moon Knight.* In these two series, the identities of Steven Grant and Jake Lockley were written out of the story. Instead, they focus on Moon Knight and Marc Spector. The other identities returned in 1998 in two mini-series written by Doug Moench, *Resurrection War,* and *High Strangeness.* However, they were not the focus of the story and were again treated as aliases. There is some discussion of Marc's mental health in *Resurrection War,* but it focuses on whether he is delusional for thinking that he had been resurrected by the Egyptian moon god Khonshu.

In the 2006 *Moon Knight* series, written by Charlie Huston, Marc's struggles with mental health came back in a big way. In the first six-issue arc of this volume, called "The Bottom," Huston shows Marc as a broken man. He has serious knee injuries, an addiction to painkillers, he's lost all his friends, and his ability to fight crime as Moon Knight. His injuries, shown in flashbacks, were the result of a climactic battle with one of his oldest foes, Bushman, in which he fell off a building. The battle ended with Moon Knight murdering Bushman by carving off his face. Over the course of this arc, he becomes Moon Knight again, to deal with a new version of The Committee.[14] In issue #5 of this series, he crashes his Moon Copter into the side of a skyscraper in New York, where The Committee is having a meeting with Taskmaster, whom they hired to kill Moon Knight. These scenes, unfortunately, lean into the negative portrayal of mental health issues, by showing Moon Knight constantly engaging in recklessly violent behaviours.

This series combined two of the worst stigmatizing tropes about DID, and mental illness in general. People with mental illness are extremely violent, and they are perpetually weak, unstable, and unable to deal with life. The face-

---

[14] The group that hired Marc to capture the *Werewolf by Night* in his very first appearance.

cutting scene has become so iconic that many fans now see it as one of the defining moments of the character. As the series went on, it continued to show a lot of graphic violence. Even though Marc was shown as trying to overcome his violent nature and not kill, he was still carving crescent moons into the foreheads of criminals. He was also shown as hitting his ex-girlfriend Marlene in a flashback and trying to win her back by stalking and physically intimidating her in the present. Eventually, he also killed again, by pushing the villain Black Spectre off the roof of a building.

Throughout this volume of *Moon Knight*, Marc is described in very harsh terms by everyone around him. In issue #4, Marlene asks him, "Are you insane? / Have you gone utterly stark raving mad?"[15] His former best friend, Jean-Paul Duchamp, wants nothing to do with him and tells his partner Rob, who is helping Marc with physical therapy, to stay away from him. When he goes to see Gena, the owner of the diner he used to frequent as Jake Lockley, she is furious because he wasn't there for her when her son died in the military. Captain America and Iron Man, who were fighting a super-hero civil war at the time, both come to Marc separately to tell him that they don't want him on their side. In issue #8, Captain America tells him, "If I have any doubts about registration, it's because of maniacs like you. / [Frank] Castle may belong in a cage, but you belong in a straitjacket. / I just don't have time to tie it around you right now."[16] In issue #12, Iron Man tells him, "No one's interested in tracking you down and dragging you in for a psych review you'll never pass."[17] Of course, it's understandable, given his extremely violent actions, and erratic and insensitive behaviour in this volume, why these people would be saying these things to him.

The problem, then, with this volume is not any inconsistency with the story itself. It's a well-crafted story, and the art by David Finch, while a bit too gory for my taste, is very detailed and dynamic. However, by portraying Marc Spector in such a negative light, issue to issue, it reflects badly on the rest of us who have DID or other serious mental illnesses. Even though it's not uncommon

---

[15] "The Bottom, Chapter Four." *Moon Knight* Vol. 5 #4 (2006). By Charlie Huston, David Finch, and Frank D'Armata.
[16] "Midnight Sun, Chapter Two." *Moon Knight* Vol. 5 #8 (2007). By Charlie Huston, David Finch, and Frank D'Armata.
[17] "Midnight Sun, Chapter Six." *Moon Knight* Vol. 5 #12 (2007). By Charlie Huston, David Finch, and Frank D'Armata.

for people with DID to have problems like substance abuse, depression, erratic and confusing behaviour, and so on, it's also possible for us to overcome these issues through therapy, learning to live a happier and more productive life. In this volume of *Moon Knight*, however, even though Marc is trying to get his life together and be a better person, he repeatedly fails. While this can sometimes happen in life, it's not just to DID systems but to anybody. Portraying someone with DID in such a hopeless way contributes to perpetuating the overly negative view that many people have of this condition.

Several years later, in 2016, another volume of *Moon Knight*, written by Jeff Lemire, portrayed a somewhat more realistic, and ultimately hopeful, depiction of DID. Unfortunately, though, this volume also contains a negative portrayal of mental health professionals. It starts with Marc Spector in a nightmarish mental asylum, where he is subjected to shock therapy and beatings from the orderlies regularly. His therapist, Dr Emmett, tells him that he was never Moon Knight, that he is an orphan and has been in the asylum since he was twelve years old. Lemire's writing, however, suggests some ambiguity as to whether this asylum is real, or a figment of Marc's imagination. In issue #2 when Marc, speaking as the Moon Knight alter, tells his therapist "Hospitals like this don't exist anymore. Mental health facilities like this are relics."[18] He's not wrong. The days of mental asylums like the one depicted in the novel and movie *One Flew Over the Cuckoo's Nest* have been over for several decades. Sadly, that doesn't stop current comics, television series, and movies from using them as the nightmare scenario of what will happen if someone perceives you as *crazy*. The truth is modern mental health facilities are a lot more civilized, both in appearance and treatment of patients. Also, patients are only admitted or kept against their will if they have proven to be a clear danger to themselves or others, not simply because they have a mental disorder. It would be unheard of, not to mention illegal, today for a child of twelve years old to be admitted and kept until adulthood just because they were diagnosed with DID.

I know this because I have been in a modern mental health facility. I voluntarily admitted myself, on the advice of my therapist, because I was struggling with an addiction to non-suicidal self-injury. I was there for about a week and a half because that's how long it took me to figure out why I had this

---

[18] "Welcome To New Egypt, Part Two." *Moon Knight* Vol 8 #2 (2016). By Jeff Lemire, Greg Smallwood, and Jordie Bellaire.

compulsion. That understanding helped me to stop doing it. Basically, I was doing it because, as a female alter sharing the body of a male named Doug, I felt like I wasn't a real person. Of course, the fact that my therapists at the time were telling me to my face that Doug was *the real one* and I was a *delusion* didn't help matters. I was never put in a straitjacket, tied to a bed, beaten up, force-fed pills, or submitted to shock therapy while I was there. My room was not an empty padded cell, but a sparsely furnished bedroom. It was fairly normal apart from none of the furniture having any sharp edges, only rounded corners. The main thing that makes looking back on that time in my life painful is the shame I felt because we had to be in there because of me and my behaviour. Doug wasn't self-harming at all, but since we live in the same body, he had to be there with me.

Although the portrayal of the mental asylum was inaccurate and stigmatizing, Lemire's representation of DID itself was a lot more accurate and positive in comparison. To begin with, he used the accurate terminology of Dissociative Identity Disorder, rather than the outdated multiple personality disorder, the completely inaccurate split personalities, or schizophrenia. Beyond that, Marc and his system were shown as trying to work through their issues and making progress in doing so, rather than spiralling out of control with violent and abusive behaviour, like in some previous volumes.

In issue #9, Lemire shows Marc attempting to integrate his alters into himself. Interestingly, Marc tried a different technique with each alter. All the techniques shown were methods we tried when we were actively trying to integrate. The final scene of that issue was particularly poignant for me. It showed a tender, emotional conversation between Steven and Marc, in which they say goodbye to each other and integrate by embracing. That reminded me so much of some of the conversations that Doug and I had when we were trying to integrate.

However, in the following issues, the alters appear to Marc again, and it becomes clear that they didn't integrate. This was true to our experience. Integration doesn't work for everyone, and it certainly didn't work for us. When we finally found a therapist who was willing to diagnose us with DID, and fully understood how to treat it, he taught us that we can learn to live as a functional multiple system. This was a huge relief to us because it meant that we didn't have to keep trying something that never worked for us. It seems that the Moon Knight system learned this lesson as well, by the end of Lemire's run.

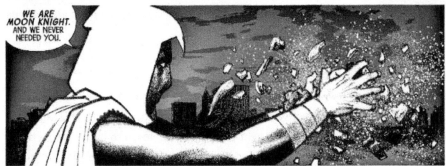

Page 16 of *Moon Knight* Vol. 8 #14.

At one point in the final issue, Marc is wandering through the desert, in a flashback to his origin as Moon Knight. He meets Steven and Jake, and asks, "Will you guys stay with me? I—I'm scared." Steven replies, "We've never left you," and Jake adds, "We've been here all along. Just rest. We're not going anywhere."[19] This is a very touching scene of the alters being there to support each other, demonstrating the best of what a DID system can be when they work together and love each other, rather than working at cross purposes. Later in the issue, when they confront Khonshu, who has been manipulating them all along, they tell him, "I am Marc Spector. I am Steven Grant. I am Jake Lockley. And we are going to be okay. We are going to live with who we are. We are Moon Knight. And we never needed you." Khonshu's skull then crumbles to dust in their hands, and for the first time in a long time, their mind is quiet and peaceful. This is such a powerful declaration of a functional multiple DID system choosing to be their best selves, and it made me very happy to read it.

These are just a few examples of how the various representations of Moon Knight throughout the years have varied in the accuracy and positivity of their portrayal of DID. I believe accuracy is very important. Most people know very little information about this disorder and learning to understand it is a key step in ending the stigma that comes with it. However, I would argue that positivity is more important. There have been so many negative portrayals of DID over the years, that it has led many people to be afraid of it, and many people who do have it to be ashamed. I believe these attitudes can lead to dire consequences such as many DID systems being too afraid to seek treatment. This in turn can lead to feeling so hopeless that they may choose to end their own life. In this way, the stigma attached to DID can potentially be fatal. This is why that stigma desperately needs to be countered with understanding, and positive, hopeful portrayals of DID in fiction. The portrayals of DID in *Moon Knight* comics are beginning to make progress in that regard, which makes me hopeful for the future. Here's hoping that it continues to get better, so that we DID systems, like Marc, Jake, and Steven, can learn to be proud of who we are, and what we have overcome together.

---

[19] "Birth and Death, Part Five." *Moon Knight* Vol. 8 #14 (2017). By Jeff Lemire, Greg Smallwood, and Jordie Bellaire.

The One You See Coming: The Art Rebirths of Moon Knight

by Jonathan Sapsed

"I'm the one you see coming." Moon Knight (MK) tells a dumbstruck hoodlum. The imposing, all-white spectral figure looming out of the night sky, his cape a billowing crescent[1]. MK is fundamentally *visual*. The character's initial appeal to readers and his uniqueness stems from the power of images and how artists have co-produced the character with the writers. MK has made several star illustrators' reputations, beginning with Bill Sienkiewicz, who casts a long shadow over later runs, but in those runs other artists have risen to the task themselves, creating outstanding visuals and storytelling. In this essay, I break

---

[1] In *Moon Knight* Vol.5. #1, "The Bottom," MK narrates a conversation he had with Hawkeye "Let me get this right, Moony. You work mostly at night? And you dress all in white? Har-dee-har-har...Told him I don't wear the white to hide myself. I wear it so they'll see me coming. So they'll know who it is. 'Cause when they see the white. It doesen't matter how good a target I am. Their hands shake so bad, they couldn't hit the moon." This is referenced again in Vol.7. #.1, "Slasher": "I got a question. Why would you wear white, and a giant cape that looks like a moon, if you're fighting crime and hunting faces at night?" "Easy. He likes people to see him coming. Because he's crazy."

Moon Knight's art history into three eras that have defined MK. Like the character's fictional story, these represent *rebirths*; distinctive artistic reinterpretations that have brought new creative possibilities.

The first of these is Sienkiewicz's 1970s/80s rendition of MK, known for his Neal Adams-inspired anatomy, but what is typically overlooked is his broader work in the run that represents the elements, air/wind, earth, light/fire, and water. These set the artistic tools for later MK stories.

The second and third are two more recent runs that have reconceptualised MK visually in the 2010s. First Declan Shalvey and Jordi Bellaire's innovations in aspects of design, including the introduction of the Mr Knight persona. Second, is Greg Smallwood's psychological journey with an ensemble cast of collaborating artists, which internalised MK's visual environment in his mindscape. These three interpretations boosted the character's popularity and influenced later runs as well as the Disney+ television series.

Bill Sienkiewicz and the Elements of Moon Knight

One of the lazy clichés in comics criticism is that Bill Sienkiewicz was a 'Neal Adams clone' throughout Moon Knight, his first series, and only began expressing himself when he moved to the New Mutants. However, this is a misrepresentation. Sienkiewicz was indeed a devoted student of Adams in those early years, learning how to deliver quality pages regularly. He has acknowledged that he used Adams' body of work as a reference "I wanted to be as good as [him] because his work looked correct."[2] If one compares Sienkiewicz's MK with Adams' figure work on another caped crusader of the night the influence is clear. Posture, the preferred foreshortening of limbs, the sparks of impact when characters punch and kick each other, even the way the ribs or knees can be seen through the costumes. To an extent, Adams was an original choice, since most artists until the 1980s had learned from earlier masters like Jack Kirby, John Buscema, or Gil Kane and this perhaps was one reason why the influence was so conspicuous, nobody was labelled a Kirby-clone or Buscema-clone because there were so many of them. The choice of Adams reflected a generational shift and as Sienkiewicz has said "As far as training and learning, I don't think I could have picked anyone better."

---

[2] Thomas, Michael. "Bill Sienkiewicz Interview." Comic Book Resources, 2001. cbr.com/bill-sienkiewicz-interview/

However, focusing only on the foundations of Sienkiewicz's MK draughtsmanship is a great disservice. In the structure that was built on those foundations, Sienkiewicz was experimenting and pushing boundaries throughout the MK run. Therefore, the transition to New Mutants was a continuation, not a step change. This is especially true of the later issues with several iconic stories and covers, but the roots can be found in earlier issues. While Sienkiewicz was growing as an artist, he was also growing the complex character of MK. This was helped by a genuine creative partnership with writer Doug Moench, who has explained "In the very beginning when the character was first introduced, there was less emphasis on the psychological stuff. He was playing the four roles and then the problems started coming up, so I delved into that. And because Bill's art is what it is, I played up a *film noir* mood."[3] Sienkiewicz's ability to create atmosphere and convey character shaped the narratives and themes of the formative years of MK.

For instance, how Sienkiewicz's page and panel designs advanced from the early stories in The Hulk magazine. He routinely used small, well-behaved rectangular panels, only varying action scenes with diagonals, or MK swinging across panel borders, or borders were dropped to make the action stand out. By issue #9 of MK's own series, Sienkiewicz is mostly using four page-wide panels per page. Varying perspectives and angles from above, below, mid-distance, and close-up. At times using the four panels for zooming in, such as MK perching on a building and peering into a window, before crashing in on the next page. The only variations of this panel structure in the issue are a vertical half-splash showing the underground web of trash that the delirious Midnight Man constructed as a bizarre gallery, and then two nine-panel grids, one shows Midnight Man at the centre shooting clockwise around the surrounding panels as MK gracefully evades the bullets until all are spent.

Other clever page designs include MK battling an adversary while trying to keep awake from Morpheus' dream state. The page shows him pricking himself with crescent darts, with thin, spike-like panels interspersed with the larger images of his fighting.[4] Another is the 'Moon Kings' story, which

---

[3] Catron, Michael. "A New Phase for Moon Knight." *Amazing Heroes* #6 (Nov 1981).
[4] "The Dream Demon." *Moon Knight* Vol. 1 #22 (1982). By Doug Moench, Bill Sienkiewicz, and Christie Scheele.

features passages in which MK is experiencing parallel narratives.[5] In reality, he is facing drugged attackers on the New York streets while hallucinating that they are horned, purple creatures he's fighting on the moon. This is shown to impressive effect in the opening splash page, split between the two scenes, with a moon background on the left complemented on the right by the curve of a subway tunnel back on earth, as MK faces the onrushing opponents.

In the story, these parallel visuals are shown through successive panels mirroring the action but with moon/mean streets figures and backgrounds. This culminates in a rapidly approaching monster, which is actually a subway train. MK cries "Marlene!"[6] as he tends to do when close to death. We cut to Marlene, who has succumbed to the crazy-making water, her face is wide-eyed and grinning, as she squats in a flooded bathroom clutching a shard of broken mirror. Chilling. Sienkiewicz has a talent for rendering crazy villains, and none more so impactful than pure souls that have been turned. This effect is reinforced on the cover of the following issue,[7] with MK himself cackling through a torn mask, stooping with flailing hands like a deranged hunchback, the werewolf villain looming triumphant behind him.

In "Moon Kings," Sienkiewicz told parallel visual stories contributing to a single narrative, a technique best shown in his most celebrated MK story, 'Hit It!'.[8] In this tale, child-like sketches of a large scary figure slapping a crying child reappear throughout the story. A recurring reminder of a violent man's memories of being abused. The visceral power of the sketchy caricatures contrasts with the rendered images of MK and the antagonist moving through the city. In addition, musicians appear throughout, linking *hitting* with *percussion*. This implies a compulsive rhythm to violence and its continuity across generations. This story Sienkiewicz considers a high point of his run and the one where he influenced the plot the most. While Moench's words also hit the beats, this issue shows their collaboration at a peak. "Hit

---

[5] "The Moon Kings." *Moon Knight* Vol. 1 #7 (1981). By Doug Moench, Bill Sienkiewicz, and Dan Warfield.

[6] Ibid.

[7] "Night of the Wolves." *Moon Knight* Vol. 1 #8 (1981). By Doug Moench, Bill Sienkiewicz, and Roger Slifer.

[8] "Hit It!" *Moon Knight* Vol. 1 #26 (1982). By Doug Moench, Bill Sienkiewicz, and Christie Scheele.

It!" is a great example of how the comic medium can express meaning and social commentary even through a genre like that of superheroes.

Apart from the innovations and imagination in storytelling, there are other recurring themes in the Moench-Sienkiewicz run. These, to varying degrees, define the character and what we see in later runs. The themes fall into natural literary *elements*, which may or may not have been a conscious choice from the creative team but may explain the instinctive appeal of the series to readers and its enduring popularity.

Air and Wind

Sienkiewicz's interpretation of the MK character is most distinguishable from Don Perlin's original design by the billowing cape, which catches the wind and allows MK to glide through the air over short distances. This is the classic Bill Sienkiewicz visual, MK descending, a white ghostly figure with only black and eye slits under the hood. The broad cape forming a crescent behind him, graceful and airy, contrasting with the weighty dark figures and structures around him. His movements seem to defy gravity and the laws of physics. Showing how, despite having no real superpowers *per se*, MK has something much stronger: artistic license. His cape crescents and buoyancy may be unlikely, but they make for iconic splash pages. The wind plays a key role in the "Spirit of the Sands,"[9] in which the Egyptian sands continually blow around and a vortex of wind mysteriously blows through the tomb of Khonshu, allowing MK to utilise his cape and swoop down on his assailant. MK and possibly Khonshu too is a force of *air and wind*.

Earth

The 'Spirit of the Sands' is disorienting because of the shifting landscape of the dunes. MK is far more used to the urban structures and natural growth of the city. These represent *Earth* in the run and MK's environment of grimy city streets. There is a lyrical beauty to Sienkiewicz's cityscapes, like the opening splash page of the "Scarlet in Moonlight" story,[10] an establishing scene of South Bronx tenements, elegantly realised through horizontal lines for the brickwork in the background. Vertical poles jut up in the foreground to hold washing lines, each laden with hanging laundry, all white against the night sky, which shows

---

[9] "Spirit of the Sands." *Moon Knight* Vol. 1 #28 (1982). By Doug Moench, Bill Sienkiewicz, and Christie Scheele.

[10] "Scarlet in Moonlight." *Moon Knight* Vol. 1 #24 (1982). By Doug Moench, Bill Sienkiewicz, and Christie Scheele.

the full moon and the intense eyes of Scarlet Fasinera, the story's antagonist. The genius here is to elevate the mundane to the sublime, and all through marks that look spontaneous but are made on a meticulous composition.

Light and Fire

The way Sienkiewicz represents light in the MK run is another intriguing way to create an atmosphere. Lights are contained in boundaries, and streetlights appear as straight-sided triangles, more like spotlights in the deep darkness, highlighting characters. While car headlights are usually roughly drawn circles, like two big discs on the front bumpers. This demonstrates their artificiality and the dominance of darkness. Lights also represent risk and danger, like Crawley jumping out in front of Lockley's cab in 'Moon Kings', his silhouette flailing ahead of bright yellow circles and the emanation of blood-red rays. This moment foreshadows MK facing the oncoming train later in the story. In his delusion, he perceives the two headlights as the eyes of a monster. The same effect is used for the light of the train that apparently runs into Scarlet in "Scarlet in Moonlight." Throughout art history, light has more often been shown as a positive force but occasionally as a symbol of danger. An example is the Spanish artist Goya's *The 3rd of May 1808 in Madrid*, also known as *The Executions*. The painting presents a luminescent man as he faces a firing squad.[11] This is the weaponised way Sienkiewicz uses light in these scenes. Such as how the villain Morpheus is finally beaten, "negated by the vicious light" when MK coaxes him to connect to a generator.[12]

Fire too is a recurring threat. From as early as Lupinar, in the Hulk magazine run,[13] lighting candles in successive small panels as he reveals his wicked plan, to then be revealed as a wolfman. Explosions also feature regularly, the one in "Assault on Island Strange"[14] Sienkiewicz represents as a burning sun, the car headlight scaled up. Fire similarly appears in several striking covers, with a burning skeleton holding a rifle on #5 and MK himself burning among the

---

[11] Collings, Matthew. *This is Civilisation*. 21 Publishing, 2008.

[12] "The Nightmare of Morpheus." *Moon Knight* Vol. 1 #12 (1981). By Doug Moench, Bill Sienkiewicz, and Christie Scheele.

[13] "Countdown to Dark." *Hulk! Magazine* Vol. 1 #14 (1979). By Doug Moench, Bill Sienkiewicz and Steve Oliff.

[14] "Assault on Island Strange." *Moon Knight* Vol. 1 #19 (1982). By Doug Moench, Bill Sienkiewicz, and Christie Scheele.

flames above a cityscape on #20. Each illuminates the key figures in dramatic elemental light.

Water

Water features in several stories in the run are often utilised as a threat. Such as in the Moon Kings/Night of the Wolves arc, in which drinking water turns the city population into maniacs. The first part climaxes with Sienkiewicz's unnerving depiction of Marlene, with all the taps overflowing in the bathroom. In "Perchance to Scream,"[15] MK is thrown into a drowning nightmare against Morpheus. His panic is obvious from streaming bubbles and the ink splatter that became a signature motif of Sienkiewicz, introduced in this run. In the Midnight Man arc, sewer water gushes onto Grant's captured butler Samuels. Sienkiewicz shows this through raking lines spattered with dirt. When MK gets under the water the lines swirl menacingly, until he can kick through the wall and the water lines all converge to convey the suction. The story's climax has MK beating Bushman in a shallow water pond in a park because water can work in MK's favour too.

There is a swimming pool entrance to Grant's mansion where he can make a dramatic entrance to surprise Marlene. She is often found lounging in the pool, naked or covered by bubbles, a sensuously wet inner core of MK's home base.

But water features most often as rain: driving lines pounding onto Jake Lockley's cab or soaking a pier at the waterfront, an atmospheric device to make moments more poignant, like the death of Marc Spector's brother Randall ("Rain continues to fall. And the blood still runs red.")[16] or Sienkiewicz's last pages in the series.[17] These show the elements taking over, with MK watching the werewolf Jack Russell run off, into streaming puddles, the last image of MK is all vertical lines and negative space as if MK has absorbed so much rain, he is subsumed into it.

Those last issues show Bill Sienkiewicz in his pomp. The inking of his own pencils shows his flair, like the famous splatter, used to show impact or just to

---

[15] "Perchance to Scream." *Moon Knight* Vol. 1 #23 (1982). By Doug Moench, Bill Sienkiewicz, and Christie Scheele.

[16] "Shadows in the Heart of the City, Part II." *Hulk! Magazine* Vol. 1 #18 (1979). By Doug Moench, Bill Sienkiewicz, and Steve Oliff.

[17] "The Moonwraith, Three Sixes, and a Beast." *Moon Knight* Vol. 1 #30 (1983). By Doug Moench, Bill Sienkiewicz, and Christie Scheele.

Page 27 of *Moon Knight* Vol. 1 #30.

dramatize skies and backgrounds. There are other textures he's able to show through cross-hatching in all directions. This is unusual for American comics, and reminiscent of the great Italian illustrator Sergio Toppi, of whom Sienkiewicz became a great admirer, but not until after this MK work.[18]

Bill would go on to New Mutants and Elektra: Assassin to great acclaim, but to those original Sienkiewicz MK fans, it felt like an exclusive club. Much of what came later was foreshadowed in the MK run, the famous Demon Bear in *New Mutants*, for example, shows much the same bestial rage we see in the werewolf in *MK* #29-30. *Elektra: Assassin* is a major artistic departure, but you can see the suffering intensity and religiosity of Scarlet as well as Marlene at times in the visual characterisation.

For MK himself Sienkiewicz's work is defining. It was a true collaboration with Doug Moench, who allowed Bill's artistic capabilities to influence his ideas of this complex character, his ensemble, and his environment. Stories that played on psychological ambiguity, and a dark tone, often with a supernatural element are the most successful and the most imitated. The iconic image of MK all in white with the crescent cape of course features in later runs, but so do the other elements. Whether with Mr Knight entering the earth, going underground in the Ellis-Shalvey run or the sandy winds in the city in Lemire-Smallwood, or Sun King's fire by Bemis. Both those last two runs end with MK in the rain, like this original. But while Sienkiewicz is the defining MK artist, this run nevertheless invites others to pick up the ideas and make their own innovations.

Declan Shalvey and Jordi Bellaire: Innovations in Design

Thirty years after the classic Moench-Sienkiewicz series came an artistic rebirth for MK, with Declan Shalvey, Warren Ellis, and colourist Jordi Bellaire. This run included several visual innovations for the character. The Shalvey run's fresh page and cover designs rebooted the character while also paying homage to prior motifs. This run was positioned as Marvel giving Ellis licence for a modern relaunch of the character with Shalvey as a promising but relative newcomer on art. Ellis insisted in interviews that his strategy was to boil

---

[18] Sienkiewicz, Bill. "Foreword." *The Collected Toppi, Vol. 1: The Enchanted World.* Magnetic Press, 2019.

down the character to its essence,[19] while Shalvey seized the opportunity to apply a new form of design sense to the series.

This approach is clear in various character designs, including MK's classic costume, to which Shalvey added solid black panels to the torso and legs, with white armour plates, and crescents over the top. This added clarity to the classic costume, which always had an ambiguity as to whether it was black or white inside the cape. Bill Sienkiewicz, with some *artistic license,* had said that despite its white appearance it was actually jet black but reflected light so as to look white.[20]

Shalvey's sleek design has been adopted by other artists and for a Marvel Legends action figure. He animated the Egyptian god Khonshu from the familiar inert stone statue to an offbeat conversational figure with an eye-catching bird skull for a head. Khonshu offers guidance and reassurance to MK, seated in Grant's mansion, all the while cobwebs stretch across his physical form.

This bird-head motif is also used for an alternative MK costume,[21] an Egyptian- / samurai-inspired armour made of bones, with a sharp and threatening beak. This all-white costume MK retrieves from old boxes of forgotten artefacts he had collected, to help him fight a gang of violent ghost punks. While he cannot land a punch on the intangible punks as Mr Knight, in the bone armour he can smack them into little punk pieces. This is carefully drawn by Shalvey, who shares the same patience and vision of David Finch in depicting violence through the detail of its effects in the moment: smash and splatter. Early in this issue Mr Knight's jacket and the skin of his back are shredded by a ghost punk's chain whip, drizzling blood across the white snow. Finch had worked on an earlier influential run written by Charlie Huston,[22] which ratcheted up the violence. Finch drew MK's costume covered with rips, blood drops, and the grime of the streets, all detailed texture, and weight. While retaining the violent aesthetics and grisly environment the Shalvey depiction instead elevated MK above it all.

---

[19] Towers,Andre. "Warren Ellis previews new inhuman based comic, Karnak." EW, 2015. ew.com/article/2015/08/24/warren-ellis-karnak-exclusive-preview/

[20] Catron, Michael. "Black or White?" *Amazing Heroes* #6 (Nov 1981).

[21] "Box." *Moon Knight* Vol. 7 #3 (2014). By Warren Ellis, Declan Shalvey, and Jordie Bellaire.

[22] *Moon Knight* Vol. 5 #1-12 (2006).

The Mr Knight character design was first introduced by Ellis in his Secret Avengers run with Michael Lark on art.[23] Marc Spector wears a simple all-white three-piece suit and balaclava. Shalvey makes this design his own, every crease in the fabric perfectly placed in his varying lines. Mr Knight struts into the first issue of this run[24] on a splash page, with physicality and intent that foreshadows the fights and victories to come. The power of the Mr Knight figure, however, also owes to the restraint of colourist Jordi Bellaire, who leaves it completely untouched against the strong and focused colour templates she deploys in these mostly night-time stories. Unlike the MK of earlier runs, which were usually tinged with a light blue by colourists like Bob Sharen, Mr Knight is simply *luminescent* against all the dirt and darkness in which he operates. Unlike the Finch portrayal of a hero stained and tarnished by his street-level world, Shalvey's ink washes and Bellaire's palettes expose him as a pure, invincible, moon spirit distinct from his environment. "I made the decision to not have him coloured or rendered with graywash so that his look could be incorporated into the book with more of an eye toward design." Shalvey has explained.[25]

Despite his innovations Shalvey's art also invoked Sienkiewicz's urban scenes capturing the moods of the city at night. He includes incidental details, like a discarded coffee cup on the ground or a branch of a tree stretching overhead. The city is shown as an ecosystem, with its occupants adapting to its artificial structures. In issue #1 Mr Knight descends through a sewer, with an ingenious page design in which Shalvey shows him climbing down the fixtures like a long vertical staircase to hell. Bellaire colours the descent an increasingly deep red. This vertical panel is overlaid on three horizontals showing a subway train at the top (with graffiti and broken tiles on the station platform). At the second level, a group of down-and-outs roast what looks like a cat over a burning drum coloured a warm amber. At the third level are pipes, cables, and the hidden underground city infrastructure we tend to forget about, coloured a greyish blue. This page design and its inking and colours fit the tone of the first issue perfectly. It works sequentially but without hard panel borders and

---

[23] "Aniana." *Secret Avengers* Vol. 1 #19 (2011). By Warren Ellis, Michael Lark, and Jose Villarrubia.

[24] "Slasher." *Moon Knight* Vol. 7 #1 (2014). By Warren Ellis, Declan Shalvey, and Jordie Bellaire

[25] Shalvey, Declan. *The Art of Declan Shalvey*. Marvel, 2019. Page 58.

conveys a snapshot cross-section of the urban underground, a recurring motif of darkness in the human psyche through this run.

At the bottom level, Mr Knight finds his prey, the slasher. He is revealed to be a former S.H.I.E.L.D. agent who has transformed himself into a cyborg living weapon through discarded S.H.I.E.L.D tech and body parts of his victims. He is a gruesome figure in the fight, pumping out blood from Mr Knight's crescent dart incisions, flailing streams, and globules in the air. The colours in this sequence are striking red, white and blue, representing the deranged patriotism of this discharged soldier. Only the yellow of his gun firing breaks this combination, which shows through eight panels the split seconds of Mr Knight deflecting the bullet back and tossing his crescent dart on the ground by the fallen slasher. This last image reoccurs in the last issue of the run, "Spectre,"[26] as Mr Knight discards a more conventional dart from Black Spectre, a disgruntled police officer who resists Mr Knight's involvement in the first issue. The panels serve as bookends to the regrettably short series.

All six stories are self-contained episodes with quite distinctive artwork. "Sniper"[27] experiments with visual storytelling, beginning with an opening sequence of eight characters in separate conversation subplots, told through eight-panel grids. The panels disappear one by one over the pages, as their corresponding characters are shot dead, leaving increasing empty space where their panels should be. This culminates in a page with one panel and empty space where seven equivalent panels have been vacated. This shows another shrewd use of the medium to tell stories with a design awareness, showing nothingness where there was life only a moment before.

The sequence leads to the title page and the introduction of MK in his classic cape, but new costume, peering down into the city, with the corpses scattered on the sidewalk outside the building where they had been working. The copter then swoops down from a bulging moon to release MK. Falling he opens his cape; a vast white crescent stretching across the page with panels overlaid, showing a pure ghost-white shape looming over the oblivious sniper. The next sequence is silent action as MK and the sniper evade each other with

---

[26] "Spectre." *Moon Knight* Vol. 7 #6 (2015). By Warren Ellis, Declan Shalvey, and Jordie Bellaire.

[27] "Sniper." *Moon Knight* Vol. 7 #2 (2014). By Warren Ellis, Declan Shalvey, and Jordie Bellaire.

grappling hooks, before the conclusion with the sniper himself shot. All this story is coloured again with a restrained grey-green palette, with the contrasting powerful use of red as the victims are shot. Efficient, direct storytelling, with three talented creators in Ellis, Shalvey, and Bellaire all working in harmony.

As well as the gritty reality of the city, this run's art also reaches heights of supernatural imagination, like the dream sequence in "Sleep."[28] This has MK exploring a fungal world of dreams, embellished with fine detail and varied forms and texture coloured with quasi-psychedelic hues so it feels more like a Steve Ditko *Dr Strange* story than the street-level MK. Shalvey's approach was influenced by the work of the French artist Phillipe Druillet, whom Ellis had recommended to Shalvey for this issue.[29]

An issue much admired by fans and critics is "Scarlet"[30] – "the perfect action comic" according to Hassan Otsmane-Elhaou, whose podcast episode of *Strip Panel Naked* focuses on the issue.[31] Mr Knight fights his way up a building despatching various thugs in brutal ways along his ascent. The *Strip Panel Naked* video demonstrates how the relative size and posture of the figures is key, where Mr Knight's antagonists progressively shrink as he bests them. In terms of fight choreography, this is paced rhythmically, and the visuals are varied and compelling, even if the script lacks some depth. Again, this builds on the Finch run, MK intimidating through violence.

It is the design approach to storytelling, page and panel layouts that is the great strength of the run. This served as a major rebirth for MK, raising interest and popularity. This is enhanced by other design choices by Shalvey and Bellaire, such as the new logo and the consistent cover designs; each with a half-page illustrating a core vision of the issue. Everything has been considered, from the cover to the closing page, which always ends with a moon crescent in the last panel.

---

[28] "Sleep." *Moon Knight* Vol. 7 #4 (2014). By Warren Ellis, Declan Shalvey, and Jordie Bellaire.

[29] Shalvey, Declan. *The Art of Declan Shalvey*. Marvel, 2019. Page 60.

[30] "Scarlet." *Moon Knight* Vol. 7 #5 (2015). By Warren Ellis, Declan Shalvey, and Jordie Bellaire.

[31] "Creating a good action comic." Strip Panel Naked. YouTube, 2016. youtu.be/KbMj9f0mcBA

Lemire, Smallwood, and the Ensemble Arc

The Ellis-Shalvey-Bellaire run was a high point for the character. However, the combination of Jeff Lemire and Greg Smallwood, retaining Jordi Bellaire's colour art kept some of the best visual aspects of the previous run, and added their own style through a 14-issue story that always kept the reader off-balance and wondering, like Marc Spector, is this really happening? The story and art portray Marc Spector's mental health struggles in ways that readers felt were accurate and sensitive, as well as driving the story's central mystery. This is the third and final artistic rebirth I analyse here.

Greg Smallwood had followed Shalvey in an earlier run with Brian Wood as writer, which teased creative storytelling through page design, including "Live,"[32] which used various forms of screens within the story also serving as sequential panels to tell it. Smallwood's illustrations for Lemire's scripts however were a level above the earlier run. The first issue[33] opens in a mental hospital, more reminiscent of Ken Kesey's *One Flew Over the Cuckoo's Nest*[34] than contemporary approaches to mental health. Lemire uses this setting as a hostile starting point for Marc Spector's psychological journey.

Smallwood expresses this through striking architectural detail, with worn and mottled hospital walls, and the sandy grit and erosion of Egyptian structures that Marc may or may not be seeing as he tries to orient himself in this space. This detail and structured background contrasts with the figures in the foreground, which are much looser and stylised, reinforcing the ambiguity of their tangibility. The hospital staff bully Marc and transform into dog-headed figures, led by Ammut, the God of judgment, who when not crocodile-headed may also be Marc's psychiatrist. Marc himself is dressed in all-white hospital garb, a nod to Shalvey and Smallwood's earlier run, with creases attentively marked through varying black lines.

The cover of the first issue shows Marc in a kind of white straitjacket, strapped and immobilised but still with an improvised cowl and crescent symbol smeared in blood. He stares through eyeholes directly at the reader, who is left with no doubt about the setting and tone of this remarkable series.

---

[32] "Live." *Moon Knight* Vol. 7 #8 (2015). By Brian Wood, Greg Smallwood, and Jordie Bellaire.

[33] "Welcome to New Egypt." *Moon Knight* Vol. 8 #1 (2016). By Jeff Lemaire, Greg Smallwood, and Jordie Bellaire.

[34] Kesey, Ken. *One Flew Over the Cuckoo's Nest*. Penguin Classics, 2005.

The pure white of Marc's clothes, along with those of the staff, is often achieved with negative space at the edge of panels, adding to the sense of lacking boundaries. As Marc's mind becomes more confused so the panels change from rectangular forms fitting the page, to panels floating in white space, or else with no panel borders at all. A recurring motif throughout the story is a page design with panels diminishing in size downward, culminating in a circle at the foot of the page, which often contains a surprise, so that the page is a literal exclamation mark. This motif is used to give Marc electric shocks through old-school mental health treatment, or a milder surprise, like introducing the unexpected Frenchie to Marc and the story.

Another clever device is the use of circles inset within panels. These act like pressure points, to focus the reader's attention, for example on Marc's hand closing to a fist or a syringe with a tranquillizer. The most brutal use of these is a series of overlaid circles showing the body impact points in a fight with the hospital orderlies. The story is replete with visual mechanics to direct the eye or signal a change in psychic level. For example, sequences of conversations with Khonshu are scratchy and smudgy renderings. Marc's notebooks from the hospital files are scribbled sketches, drawn by Lemire rather than Smallwood, to show the change of voice. They feel like a nod to Sienkiewicz's 'Hit It' childish doodles discussed above.

Ironically considering Smallwood's quality throughout this run, one of its highest artistic achievements had him play a less obvious role. The arc through issues #5 to 9 saw three parallel stories featuring the MK personas, each illustrated by a different artist: Stephen Grant producing an MK movie in Hollywood, drawn by Wilfredo Torres; Jake Lockley driving his cab through New York, drawn by Francesco Francavilla; and an MK astronaut fighting wolfmen in space, drawn by James Stokoe. It is not uncommon for artists to share the work of single issues, usually to ease the main artist's workload, but it is rare to see it done in such a designed and accomplished manner that adds, rather than subtracts to the storytelling.

Smallwood has explained[35] that he had always planned stylistic differences for this arc when his run with Lemire was estimated to last 12 issues. When the

---

[35] "Retrospective: Greg Smallwood interview." Into the Knight Podcast, 2019. itkmoonknight.com/2020/12/15/retrospective-greg-smallwood-interview-june-2019/

run was extended, he felt he needed help to be able to deliver on the extra material but saw it as an opportunity to involve artists that matched the styles he imagined. He gave a list of possible illustrators to editor Jake Thomas who sourced the extended art team. While Smallwood still provided layouts and designs of characters and objects the three guests all delivered the perfect aesthetics for their storylines. Francavilla's loose and shady work fitted the urban sequences centred around Lockley's cab and the grime and fumes of New York, with dialogue from Lemire that seemed straight from Martin Scorsese's *Taxi Driver*. This was a vast contrast with Stokoe's lunar werewolves' story (surely a nod and a wink to Moench-Sienkiewicz's "Moon Kings" as well as the Lupinar character in the early "Countdown to Dark" story[36]), including the intricate detail of spacecraft, stations, suits, and weapons that he is known for in his *Aliens* work and his flair for monsters shown in Orc Stain.[37] Both these subplots were coloured with distinctive palettes by their respective artists; more gradated pastels in Stokoe's space sequences, with blocks of flat purples, reds, oranges, and blues from Francavilla in Lockley's street level. Torres' plotline with Grant meanwhile showed a more glamorous Hollywood setting with the beautiful and rich people surrounding Grant and Marlene, coloured sympathetically by Michael Garland.

These three arcs pursue their own agendas, but their core protagonists, the fractured personas of Marc Spector, try to make sense of and ultimately escape the worlds in which they find themselves. Along the way there are incursions between the parallel plots; space pilot MK's crescent spaceship is shot down simultaneously with Lockley crashing his cab. Grant becomes aware there is a moon-based movie being staged on the adjacent set, and suddenly feels the bite on his neck from the wolf Lupinar from that other world. The pace of the rotation between the stylised plots increases as the characters rush to an exit at the end of "Incarnations."[38] Finally, all three enter another exclamation mark page, to be welcomed by Marc Spector, in Mr Knight's suit, but with a plaster across the bridge of his nose, denoting his wounds and mood for recovery. Looking sheepish he says, "Hey fellas…thanks for coming…we need to talk." This

---

[36] "Countdown to Dark." *Hulk! Magazine* Vol. 1 #14 (1979). By Doug Moench, Bill Sienkiewicz, and Steve Oliff.

[37] Stokoe, James. *Orc Stain* Vol. 1 #1-7 (2010).

[38] "Incarnations." *Moon Knight* Vol. 8 #8 (2016). By Jeff Lemaire, Greg Smallwood, and Jordie Bellaire.

difficult conversation leads to a disintegration of the three entrants and a re-integration of Marc Spector's mind.

The way in which these subplots interchange, frequently on the same page, at times feels disruptive but not disjointed, and at other points smooth and segued. As a representation of a fractured mind trying to protect and heal itself, it is a technical masterpiece of sequential art storytelling that Lemire, Smallwood and the team were able to achieve, and according to Smallwood with no coordination hitches or miscommunications. Presumably, however, the scripting, briefing, and preparation of the wider team by the core creators enabled this fluid execution.

The final arc of the run reassembles some of these devices, with Smallwood returning solo. In "Birth and Death,"[39] Mr. Knight tries to renegotiate the deal for Crawley's soul. He flies into space, across a double-page spread, gliding over remembered utterings from his troubled medical history, then he is upside-down, tumbling through space, finally landing, only to be attacked by Egyptian warriors riding giant ants. These last issues are interspersed with sequences from Marc's origin and biography. Like the parallel personas, these subplots are coloured radically different by Bellaire to distinguish them.

Again, the pace of the story builds to a climax, "Birth and Death, Part 5"[40] has seven pages of wide-screen four-panel grids, which culminate in Marc, Stephen, Jake, and Moon Knight crushing the ossified bird skull of Khonshu, symbolising the release from his influence. The last three pages show Marc at peace, gazing over the city, absorbing the rain (another nod to Sienkiewicz's elements). A perfect end to a masterful collaborative story. If it was not Intellectual Property-driven comics, this ending could be an ideal conclusion to the MK character's story, as it is, it serves as another rebirth.

Conclusions

This chapter has focused on the work of artists in co-creating the character and context of MK, which is not to say that writers have not been important, but rather that the visual aspects of character design, movement, mood, and storytelling have contributed arguably more to MK than less complex

---

[39] "Birth and Death, Part One." *Moon Knight* Vol. 8 #10 (2017). By Jeff Lemaire, Greg Smallwood, and Jordie Bellaire.

[40] "Birth and Death, Part Five." *Moon Knight* Vol. 8 #14 (2017). By Jeff Lemaire, Greg Smallwood, and Jordie Bellaire.

characters. The three runs all redesigned the MK character and left lasting iconography and narrative depth that have been picked up by subsequent publications as well as the Disney+ MK television series. The rich tools and elemental tropes were set out by Bill Sienkiewicz. Declan Shalvey developed the Mr Knight persona and brought a design sensibility to the series. Jeff Lemire and Greg Smallwood experimented with the interior life of MK with pioneering sequential storytelling.

These artists and runs were selected because they all advanced the character artistically and in storytelling, which is not to underestimate Don Perlin's original design of the anti-werewolf villain in MK's introduction, nor other supremely talented artists like Alex Maleev, David Finch, Jacen Burrows, Paul Davidson and Tomm Coker who have drawn the character. At the time of writing Alessandro Cappuccio, the current MK artist is offering another distinctive vision of *the one you see coming.* The multi-layered nature of the character is that there are likely to be more rebirths and interpretations to see yet.

The Spector at Work: Moon Knight as a Metaphor for the Workplace

by Emmet O'Cuana

"Every day I invent a name to live inside" – Sean Bonney[1]

"I am not Marc Spector."
">sigh< No? Who are we today, then, Marc? Jake Lockley? Steve Grant?"
"I am the Moon Knight. I am the Fist of Khonshu."[2]

Marc Spector is dead.

The superhero Moon Knight is a masked vigilante who hunts criminals at night. He is a sometime member of the Avengers. He is a reluctant priest of the Egyptian god Khonshu. He is a werewolf hunter. He is mentally ill. He is also – billionaire playboy Steven Grant, gossip-loving cabbie Jake Lockley, and the

---

[1] Bonney, Sean. "Confessional Poetry." *Blade Pitch Control Unit*. Salt Publishing, 2005.
[2] "Welcome to New Egypt: Part Two." *Moon Knight* Vol 8 #2 (2016). By Jeff Lemire, Greg Smallwood, and Jordie Bellaire.

mysteriously resurrected mercenary Marc Spector, a man who died in a tomb in Sudan.

Moon Knight encompasses all of this (and no doubt my fellow writers in this collection have already introduced you to his many identities). He is seen as a *lunatic* by his fellow superheroes, or paratextually by certain creative teams or commenters on the comic as suffering from Dissociative Identity Disorder (DID). This diagnosis is officially canon, as of Jeff Lemire's run. However, Lemire goes further, exploring how Marc's madness is an almost logical response to the oppression he encounters and is controlled by.

I am interested in this as being analogous to Deleuze and Guattari's schizoanalysis[3] of the contemporary worker. As they observe in *Anti-Oedipus: Capitalism and Schizophrenia*, psychoanalysis recategorized mythic archetypes and forms as subjective psychological experiences or higher-order symbols of the individual unconscious mind. Deleuze and Guattari describe this as a *privatization* of the individual self, creating a more pliable labourer, concerned with their desires and self-interest, in opposition to the needs and requirements of an exterior world (workplace trade unionism, community action, environmental activism).

"Consequently, the ambiguity of psychoanalysis in relation to myth or tragedy has the following explanation: psychoanalysis undoes them as objective representations, and discovers in them the figures of a subjective universal libido [...] Psychoanalysis does treat myth and tragedy, but it treats them as the dreams and the fantasies of private man"[4]

To this formula, they propose a *schizoanalysis*, a rejection of both conservative values, psychoanalysis and capitalism. In Lemire's vision of Moon Knight, I note an embrace not only of the character's mythic heritage as the priest of an Egyptian god but of his insanity, rejecting the pathologizing of Marc Spector by previous creative teams.

Overall, Moon Knight's quite a slippery character and difficult to categorise. However, he is useful as a metaphor for how we exist within the workplace. As Marc, Steven and Jake bounce between their different jobs, so too are we as employees in the 21st century, encouraged to *hustle* outside of our main

---

[3] Deleuze, Gilles and Felix Guattari. *Anti-Oedipus: Capitalism and Schizophrenia*, Penguin Classics, 2009.
[4] Ibid.

sources of employment to afford the rising cost of living. There is something very recognizable in the character who races around his city changing out of clothes, risking his mental health and serious injury due to sleep deprivation and constant physical demands on his body.

This essay will describe the points of connection between navigating the contemporary reality of employment and work while wearing multiple hats, and how Moon Knight attempts the same with his superhero career.

Oh, Superman

To discuss the function of Moon Knight as a metaphor for our relationship to the workplace, we need to touch on the metaphorical power of the superhero idea itself. This leads us to the codifier of the superhero genre – Superman. Contradicting Frank Miller's definition of the superhero genre as a revolt by Jerry Siegel and Joe Shuster against the status quo, represented by landlords, bankers, and corrupt politicians,[5] Umberto Eco's *The Myth of Superman* describes how Superman became a guardian of those same forces of control.[6] Superman is the originator of many aspects of the superhero, be it the moral code these vigilantes and mythic heroes live by, and indeed their choice of costume (a cape, an emblem, rigidly defined colour coordination). In Eco's view, he has also become a conservative fantasy of social control.

Observing the contradiction of Superman's limited civic and political action in contrast to his sheer omnipotence and capacity to transform the world, Eco notes "[as] evil assumes only the form of an offence to private property, good is represented only as charity. This simple equivalent is sufficient to characterise Superman's moral world."[7]

Superheroes following the model of Kal El, a.k.a. Clark Kent (multiple identities is another superhero codifier, Marc is simply more committed to the bit), tolerate the indignity of modern living. The widespread inequality and

---

[5] "Go back to the origins of Superman before World War II. He was dragging generals to the front of the battles. He was fighting corrupt landlords. He was not the symbol of the status quo he's since become." Quoted in "Batman and the Twilight of the Idols: an Interview with Frank Miller" from Christopher Sharrett's *Many More Lives of the Batman* (BFI Palgrave, 2015).

[6] Eco, Umberto. "The Myth of Superman." *Arguing Comics: Literary Masters on a Popular Medium*. Ed. Jeet Heer and Kent Worcester. University Press of Mississippi, 2004.

[7] Ibid.

suffering due to limited resources for the vast majority of humankind. *Changing the world* is typically the province of the supervillain. What does that tell us? The hero defends the status quo, sometimes directly serving at the whim of an elected world leader. Frank Miller has Superman do just this in *The Dark Knight Returns* as a sign of how degraded he has become in the book's dark vision of the future. In short, Miller came to agree with Eco, superheroes are conservative fantasies.

Good Night, Moon Knight

I find Moon Knight useful as a character in opposition to the process of comic book *gentrification* objected to by Miller and presented as *a priori* by Eco. The character's essential C-list status, a reputed Batman knock-off with mental health issues, makes him less likely to be a spokesman for the status quo. Even in his first solo adventure in *Marvel Spotlight* Moon Knight seems frustrated by his own strange approach to superhero work: "Action twice in one night...these schizo quick changes are wearing me out..."[8]

Perhaps it is significant that in his original introduction in *Werewolf-By-Night* issues #32 and #33, Moon Knight is a more conventional antagonist for the title character Jack Russell (yes, that's what they went with). He first appears on the page as a costumed vigilante (silvered duds at that) for hire, paid for by a cabal of businessmen, The Committee. He ultimately turns on his employers and joins forces with the crazed werewolf – and ever since Moon Knight has been on the side of the freaks.

Moon Knight is narratologically rich. He is too morally compromised as a former mercenary to be a paragon of virtue like Eco's Parsifalian Superman. He is also not reactionary enough to be a Frank Miller antihero, like his Batman, destined to become an enemy of the US government in the dystopic futuristic 1986 of *The Dark Knight Returns*.

After his brief career as a werewolf hunter, Moon Knight, and his civilian alters Steven Grant and Jake Lockley, are revealed to be responding to the whims of an Egyptian god, Khonshu. While he is financially well-off on the back of his mercenary blood money, his shifts from a well-to-do guest at the mayor's mansion to a tardy cab driver, who enjoys drinking bad coffee and gossiping at

---

[8] "The Crushing Conquer Lord." *Marvel Spotlight* Vol. 1 #28 (1976). By Doug Moench and Don Perlin.

Gena's well-named greasy spoon café *The Other Place* (in the same evening!), show him to be effortlessly mutable along class lines.

Now credit where credit is due, three years before Moon Knight bumped into a werewolf, Dennis O'Neil, Irv Novick and Dick Giordano introduced the character of Matches Malone in *Batman* #242. Matches is a lowlife confronted by Batman who panics and accidentally kills himself. The Caped Crusader then takes the interesting step of assuming Matches' identity, a tactic he returns to repeatedly over the years. This suggests that Moon Knight and Batman are not only similar in their taste for costumes but that one could map Steven onto Bruce, and Jake onto Matches.

O'Neil would go on to edit Moench/Sienkiewicz's 1980s run on *Moon Knight*, ensuring social realist themes and commentary on life on the wrong side of the tracks, and political corruption would continue to feature in the comic. Marc's ultimate superpower, it could be argued, is that he is not locked into the perspective of a single social class.

A Spectre is Haunting the Workplace[9]

Superman, Batman, Spider-man, and Iron Man work alongside the government and business. They are compliant citizens, or sometime vigilantes *who get results*! But they never threaten the standing social order. They can even die and be resurrected multiple times because their stories have continuing commercial value. They will largely return to the land of the living unchanged, after a brief period of readjustment. Where I find Moon Knight the character useful is as a metaphor for the 21st-century labourer. Our very own precariat[10] superhero, caught in a net of confusing roles and the whims of his *employer* Khonshu.

---

[9] Engels, Friedrich and Karl Marx. *Manifesto of the Communist Party*. Marx/Engels Internet Archive (marxists.org), 1987, 2000.

[10] "The precarious class, or precariat, is distinguished as a social class by virtue of its actual comportment within (and as a result of) capitalist society. The precariat is not told that it is (nor does it need to be described as) precarious, for its precarity is a measurable feature of its life. Simply put, the precariat is the class of people who lead precarious lives, whose everyday life is set within an ongoing state of anxiety about an increasingly uncertain future." – Richard Gilman-Opalsky, *Specters of Revolt: On the Intellect of Insurrection and Philosophy from Below* (Repeater Books, 2016).

Moon Knight could legitimately die (in fact, he has, that's his origin) and never return. Years of speculation surrounding a Moon Knight movie probably saved Marc's life. The stay of execution was provided by the recent Disney+ series featuring a very charismatic performance by Oscar Isaac.

It can be argued that Moon Knight the comic book character has less exchange value than Moon Knight the television series superhero, played by a well-respected actor. In fact, the Disney+ show is the very outcome that an IP like Moon Knight is kept in circulation for, with the attendant potential multimedia growth. It is the commercial value of Moon Knight as an owned property that keeps him alive, not the importance of his story, or appeal to his niche fandom (within which I count myself a member).

Cancellation and reboots have dogged the character for most of his time in publication. Metaphorically, Moon Knight is the office worker who could vanish one week and be replaced by a compliant temp the next.

Fascinatingly the aforementioned Disney+ show not only featured a standout central performance (as well as an intriguing antagonist, the obscure character Arthur Harrow played by Ethan Hawke), but the series is also concerned with Spector's own thoughts on being a private individual and labourer. When the series begins, we are introduced to Steven Grant, a low-ranking English employee of the National Art Gallery. Despite his clear passion for Egyptian mythology (and an unusually spacious London loft apartment), Grant is mostly occupied by menial tasks in the stockroom and condescended to by his manager.

The plot begins when Khonshu (voiced by F. Murray Abraham) begins reasserting his control over the Moon Knight identity. The audience, and Steven, eventually learn that this life in London has been created for him by the original personality, Marc Spector, a retirement of sorts to live a normal life as a lowly employee. *Steven* is a tribute to Spector's deceased younger brother Randall. Spector subsumed his own identity to allow *Steven/Randall* to live an ordinary life. Randall died in a childhood accident, and Marc Spector is tortured by guilt that he happened to be resurrected by a god when he died as an adult soldier of fortune. Why shouldn't he die and give his dead brother a new life?

Essentially Spector enacted his own form of repression, both psychoanalytic and economic. Only for Khonshu (and we learn, a Spanish-speaking Jake Lockley) to reject this retreat from his real self into a parody fiction of a *work/life* in London (amusingly represented in the show by Budapest). Khonshu/Jake/Moon Knight forces the destruction of Marc's life as Steven

Grant. As Deleuze and Guattari state "[S]chizoanalysis must devote itself with all its strength to the necessary destructions. Destroying beliefs and representations, theatrical scenes. And when engaged in this task no activity will be too malevolent,"[11] No precarious life as a wage slave for him, Moon Knight is a superhero who confronts madness and myth!

Moon Knight as Code-Switching

So, here's Moon Knight, relatively obscure, replaceable, and outdistanced by fellow Marvel characters. What makes him special? How exactly is he more than a photo-negative image of Batman?

While I am not planning to compare and contrast specific creative teams and how they approached *Moon Knight* differently, between Doug Moench and Don Perlin's original run, and Jeff Lemire and Greg Smallwood's recent commercially and critically successful interpretation, Moon Knight ran the gamut from a superhero with multiple aliases and lifestyles funded by his work as a mercenary, to a psychiatric hospital patient trapped within a series of delusional states.

I am interested in broadly describing the function of Spector's multiplying self. Over the years creators have added to or taken from this complex tapestry of indvidualit(y)ies expressed by Moon Knight.

- He is the repentant revenant Marc Spector, who serves as the avatar of the god Khonshu, after dying during a botched mercenary mission.
- He is the millionaire playboy Steven Grant, comfortable hobnobbing with the social elite.
- He is Jake Lockley, a cab driver with eyes and ears on the street to aid in his fight against criminals and corrupt upper-class members.

His situational self, code-switching depending on the circumstances he finds himself in, is what makes Spector/Grant/Lockley dynamic as a masked avenger character. And given my use of the phrase code-switching, I should make a passing note that Oscar Isaac's performance in Moon Knight manages to align Spector, Grant, and Lockley along distinct cultural identities also, from Jewish American Chicagoan to lower-middle-class Englishman and finally possibly Galician Spanish-speaking hitman.

---

[11] Deleuze, Gilles and Felix Guattari. *Anti-Oedipus: Capitalism and Schizophrenia.* Penguin Classics, 2009.

Moon Knight's complexity is what sets him apart from the superhero with that ephemeral work/life balance. A balance that allows them to retreat from their punch clock escapades to a domestic existence. Moon Knight can be taken as a symbol for our own complex existences within and around our various real, professional, and virtual selves in the 21st century. It is clear how untenable his activities as a superhero are, to the point of his being considered a lunatic by his peers. Finally, almost naturally, he begins the Lemire/Smallwood run committed to an anachronistic psychiatric hospital, which, we learn, was deliberately staged by Khonshu to make Marc a vessel to be possessed (or indeed, a more pliable employee).

Mark Fisher's *capitalist realism*, as well as Ursula K. Le Guin's speech at the National Book Awards in New York in 2014, "We live in capitalism, its power seems inescapable — but then, so did the divine right of kings"[12] apply here. The superhero as a character protects and perpetuates the capitalist reality, we live in.

Many of the most notable superheroes are beneficiaries of inherited wealth and capitalist profiteering, including Tony Stark's Iron Man and Bruce Wayne's Batman. Where the superhero is not independently wealthy, they often enjoy the benefit of having cordial relationships with their billionaire Avengers or Justice League members. Benefits can include being able to access such things as equipment and free housing.

Moon Knight is notable for creeping out his peers with his schizoid splintering in response to the capitalist system they so readily protect. He's also, due to his work in black ops and as a mercenary for hire, a member of the nouveau riche. This is possibly a reason for the disdain he is treated with by the masked aristocrats he is acquainted with in the superhero community.

I also see Spector's adaptability mapping onto how we, as individuals, divide our approach to the workplace or are expected to by our corporate-aligned superego Khonshu. This is where capitalist realism and ancient Egyptian magic are shown to be analogous, equally fused into every aspect of life.

Ernst Cassirer makes the observation that in Ancient Egypt a person's name can either disguise or reveal, in the mythic sense, one's true self, which is apt

---

[12] Le Guin, Ursula K. *Speech in Acceptance of the National Book Foundation Medal for Distinguished Contribution to American Letters*. ursulakleguin.com, 2014. www.ursulakleguin.com/nbf-medal

given Spector's split into Grant and Lockley. 'And in Egypt, too, we find a similar conception, for there the physical body of man was thought to be accompanied, on the one hand, by his Ka, or double, and, on the other, by his name, as a sort of spiritual double. And of all these three elements it is just the last mentioned which becomes more and more the expression of a man's "self," of his "personality."'[13]

Moon Knight and Emotional Labour

> I like you much better as a millionaire.
>
> — Marlene, Moon Knight's love interest[14]

Even within a single role (assuming you do not have to take on side-gigs to pay your bills) your workplace persona can exist simultaneously as the obedient employee, attentive to a manager or team leader's direction; the supportive colleague to a fellow employee in distress (most likely due to the same hierarchy we comport ourselves to without outward complaint); the lunchroom gossip, indirectly or otherwise causing harm to colleagues we might be expected to be in solidarity with; and of course the public face of the organisation itself, taking care not to complain too much in polite company or on social media, more out of fear of losing employment than genuine loyalty.

Amelia Horgan's *Lost in Work* quotes Mareile Pfannebecker and James A. Smith on how "social media is a continuously rolling modelling portfolio, show-reel and curriculum vitae."[15] Now work travels with us on our devices. We are always, on some level, engaged in the workplace. Our time outside our place of employment is being eaten away. We voluntarily purchased cells in Jeremy Bentham's Panopticon.[16]

---

[13] Cassirer, Ernst. *Language and Myth*. Dover Publications, 1953.

[14] "Embassy of Fear." *Hulk!* Vol. 1 #12 (1978). By Doug Moench, Keith Pollard, Frank Giacoia, Mike Esposito.

[15] Horgan, Amelia. *Lost in Work*. Pluto Press, 2021.

[16] From the Greek *panoptes*, Bentham's solution to the problem of disciplining imprisoned convicts was to give a single guard total powers of surveillance of a prison's population. His 1791 essay "Panopticon, or the Inspection House" was perhaps most prominently popularised in the 20th century by Michel Foucault's *Discipline and Punish* (1975).

Note, I have not listed the solidarity of a union member, an option for employees that is increasingly unavailable, or discouraged.[17] Ironically, the Avengers and Justice League enjoy the fellowship and collective strength of a union. Even taking a united stand against government interference when required, while also earning billions in our world's box office sales for corporations that work to undermine union action and worker solidarity.

Perhaps there is no more illustrative example of how the contemporary workplace extorts emotional labour from its workforce than the phrase "think of the company as your family."[18] This blurring of our personal lives and the workplace was made overt during the COVID-19 pandemic lockdowns and working from home. This speaks to Moon Knight's own Russian Doll existence, crisscrossing lines of class and states both mystical and psychological.

Think of a colleague on a Zoom call having to switch between their personas as an employee and the parent who is suddenly called upon by a child. I recently undertook an orientation course for a job that cheerfully remarked such interruptions 'could become the next viral video!' Your home life could be monetized, isn't that great?!

When Marlene grows frustrated by Jake Lockley standing her up for her date with Steven Grant, Moench plays it for laughs. But in Lemire and Smallwood's run, the confusion of selves has completely overridden Marc's individuality.

What is happening to us in the breakdown of any divide between the workplace and our home lives/personal life outside of work? Is the erosion of our private selves, and the directing of our personal energies entirely towards work? Which is the perfect set of ingredients for increased levels of mental illness?

"We can have access to the modalities of digital telecommunications from everywhere and at all times, and in fact, we have to, since this is the only way to participate in the labour market. We can reach every point in the world but,

---

[17] "For as long as there have been trade unions there have been attempts to restrict them, often involving violence, imprisonment, and legal restrictions on workers' ability to join together." – Amelia Horgan, *Lost in Work* (Pluto Press, 2021).

[18] Adams, Tristram Vivian. *The Psychopath Factory: How Capitalism Organises Empathy*. Repeater Books, 2016.

more importantly, we can be reached from any point in the world. Under these conditions, *privacy* and its possibilities are abolished."[19]

Tell Me a Story

Companies can be unstable, but people cannot.
— Christian Salmon[20]

"Relax, it's not like we're saving lives" is a pithy way to dismiss white-collar work stress. Yes, whole careers in the private and public sectors involve chasing up email chains, long meetings with stakeholders that achieve little beyond allocating tasks to lower-paid employees, and management of resources somehow being described as leadership. In the proper perspective, these actions seem nebulous as a work activity. However, they are a source of tremendous stress.[21] Largely the stress and anxiety of such work are informed not by the work itself, but by the potential risk to one's financial status of losing employment.

An office worker in a corporation or government bureaucracy may not be literally saving lives, but for the purpose of their status as employees, subject to KPIs and annual reviews etc., you might forgive them for acting as if they were.

In part, this is down to the story we tell ourselves about our careers, our colleagues, and our place of work. It is the occupation of our daily allotment of time. Macbeth's 'petty pace' is the measure of our lives, spent in the blue light of a computer monitor, risking RSI as we tap away. Despite the driven nature of contemporary work, it is also weirdly purposeless.

Again COVID-19 proved to be a fascinating dilemma for the office workplace. In a single Gordian stroke remote work eliminated much of the need for middle-management roles. Staff completed their tasks, logged their work, avoided the need for a commute, and management... seemed oddly insistent on the need to return to the office workplace. The suspicion became widespread that a large amount of white-collar work simply did not matter, outside of generating reasons for management to justify their higher wages and status.

---

[19] Berardi, Franco. *The Soul at Work*. The MIT Press, 2009.
[20] Salmon, Christian. *Storytelling: Bewitching the Modern Mind*. Verso Books, 2017.
[21] See Eva Illouz's *Cold Intimacies: The Making of Emotional Capitalism* (2007) for an accounting of how "emotional transactions" became the bedrock of corporate worker management theory.

My interest here, and how I would relate it to *Moon Knight* the comic, is the idea that work has become an all-consuming story that we tell ourselves. This story, this focus of our day-to-day lives, underpins more of our existence than we might expect. Khonshu is in the habit of reminding Marc that his existence is entirely dependent on the god's interest in him. Khonshu berates Moon Knight for his failures while institutionalised in the manner of an office middle manager employing negative reinforcement.[22]

Moon Knight, let's not forget, is the priest of a god of scribes and stories. He is aware of how a good story can change your perspective of who he is, hence Moench's scripts presenting Marc, Jake and Steven as distinct personas treated by other members of the comic book's cast, Marlene, his butler Samuels, and pilot Frenchie, as separate individuals.

For example, in *Marvel Two-In-One* #52 (1979), a masked Moon Knight is rebuffed by The Thing, so he becomes his cab-driving persona Jake Lockley to be more trustworthy to the working-class Fantastic Four superhero. The story ends with this pithy exchange:

> "I just wanna know how I'm gonna get back to Manhattan. I can never find a cab at this time of night!'
>
> 'Somehow, Grimm, I don't think you'll have any problem tonight... No problem at all!'

Stories Trump Facts

In Christian Salmon's *Storytelling: Bewitching the Modern Mind* the author shares journalist Ron Suskind's anecdote of a Bush administration aide annoyed at media coverage:

"The aide said that guys like me were 'in what we call the reality-based community,' which he defined as people who 'believe that solutions emerge from your judicious study of discernible reality.' I nodded and murmured something about enlightenment principles and empiricism. He cut me off. 'That's not the way the world really works anymore,' he continued. 'We're an empire now, and when we act, we create our own reality. And while you're studying that reality—judiciously, as you will—we'll act again, creating other new realities, which you can study too, and that's how things will sort out.

---

[22] "Welcome to New Egypt: Part One." *Moon Knight* Vol. 8 #1 (2016). By Jeff Lemire, Greg Smallwood and Jordie Bellaire.

We're history's actors...and you, all of you, will be left to just study what we do."[23]

Salmon describes this as a 'fictional Realpolitik'. Governments from this point on would not have to be subject to factual analysis. Any analysis would be impossible, beyond reporting on the disruptive propaganda served up to media outlets by press officials. Yet, this is what has happened, and what is *true* for government administrations, is *true* for corporations, and is *true* of the tax-avoiding billionaire class, sorry, job creators. Stories generate subjective responses (separate realities) to the world we live in. Without a factual grounding in the Real, any sense of universal values or kinship, collective action, becomes impossible.[24]

Salmon quotes Suskind describing the 'reality-based community' comment as an attack on the institution of factual journalism.

In the past two decades, we have seen this process escalate to include the idea of citizenship itself. The rights of the citizen, without protection from the democratic state and the media of a factual accounting of the abuses of powerful individuals and corporations, are up in the air. The accelerating vulnerability of ethnic groups and migrants in Western countries. For example, President Trump's Muslim ban in the United States, the citizenship of Windrush families[25] being revoked under then Home Secretary Theresa May, or indeed asylum seekers detained offshore and in detention centres in Australia under the Scott Morrison government. These all speak to the disruption of the narrative. Their stories of suffering matter less to the voting public.

---

[23] Salmon, Christian. *Storytelling: Bewitching the Modern Mind*. Verso Books, 2017.

[24] Jean Baudrillard argues in *Simulacra and Simulation* (University of Michigan Press, 1994) that simulation has replaced representation across art, science and politics. Objective reality – the Real - has collapsed into the "imaginary" without a fixed frame of reference: "[i]t is... the map that precedes the territory – precession of simulacra – that engenders the territory." Christian Salmon further advances this idea with his exploration of storytelling trumping facts and direct hierarchical responsibility in the workplace.

[25] "There is a very specific violence that even after years of public service, including looking after some of the most vulnerable in society, Caribbean migrants of the Windrush generation (arriving between 1948 and 1973) were denied access to benefits, to healthcare, and even deported." – Amelia Horgan, *Lost in Work* (Pluto Press, 2021).

Why do we empathise with the suffering of refugees, the discriminated against, or the most vulnerable? They are the Other. The more ranks that are added to this army of othered humans, the less any possible unity in the face of authoritarianism is possible. This has consequences for us in the workplace too, with the susceptibility of our colleagues and managers, to looking the other way when faced with dehumanising policy. Step by step, we move further away from the Enlightenment ideal of the individual citizen (an individual among individuals) and become human resources, to be managed.

I is an Other[26]

Lemire and Smallwood's *Moon Knight* run positions the god Khonshu as the principal antagonist of their story, fracturing and divorcing Marc Spector's sense of reality. Unable to perceive what is real. Trapped in a psychiatric hospital and tormented by visions of Egyptian gods. Marc's struggle is to reconnect with the particulars of his past self, his distinct individuality. His life before dying in Sudan, his Judaism, and ties to his Rabbi father, are shown to be anchors to a true, factual reality that resists the schizoid stories Khonshu uses to torment him (or are a feature of his mental illness resulting from his experiences as a mercenary for hire).[27]

Marc's attempts to determine what is and is not real are rejected by Dr Emmet (a.k.a. the god Ammut) as a manifestation of his mental illness:

> "Moon Knight" is your fantasy. You've been keeping a journal of his "adventures" since you were a boy. They are delusions, Marc.
>
> It never happened, none of it. It's all been in your head.
>
> You are Marc Spector. You are an orphan. You have D.I.D., Dissociative Identity Disorder.[28]

In the face of such confounding unreality, from our algorithmically driven mobile devices to the television news, the looming Anthropocene

---

[26] From French: "Je est un Autre." Gilles Deleuze quotes this Rimbaud line in his essay "On Four Poetic Formulas that Might Summarise the Kantian Philosophy" (*Essays Critical and Clinical*, trans. Daniel W. Smith and Michael A. Greco, Verso Books, 1998).

[27] "Psychopathy is, under capitalism, not a malady but a condition that can be harnessed for profit." — Tristram Vivian Adams, *The Psychopath Factory: How Capitalism Organises Empathy* (Repeater Books, 2016).

[28] "Welcome to New Egypt: Part One." *Moon Knight* Vol. 8 #1 (2016). By Jeff Lemire, Greg Smallwood and Jordie Bellaire.

environmental apocalypse, and yes, the day-to-day anxieties and stresses of the workplace we attend to, enable us to pay bills, and purchase food and clothing, wouldn't it be reasonable for us all to go a little mad?

Mad at Work

> We are dealing with an invasion of immortals from another dimension, and we are on the clock, people. Let's rock.[29]

Marc's solution, initially at the urging of Khonshu during his manipulations of Marc, but by the run's conclusion fully embraced by Spector, is to trust in his madness.

From page 4 of *Moon Knight* Vol. 8 #2 (2016). ("It's actually English, although the Irish are fond of naming their children after failed revolutionary Robert Emmet.")

Reduced to a powerless captive by Dr Emmet/Ammut, Marc escapes the fantasy of the psychiatric hospital once he embraces his nature as a schizoid man, *Mr Knight*. When masked he insists that his companions Marlene, Crowley, Gena, and Frenchie refer to him as such. The situational codeswitching stops, but the alters are shown to be present along with Marc. Lemire's scripts

---

[29] "Welcome to New Egypt: Part Two." *Moon Knight* Vol. 8 #2 (2016). By Jeff Lemire, Greg Smallwood and Jordie Bellaire.

introduce internal conflicts, or psychomachy, between Steve, Jack and Marc. Ultimately it is in his rejection of Khonshu as a god/master that Moon Knight is shown to have embraced his mental illness and acknowledged his identity.

The 2016-2017 *Moon Knight* run features Mr Knight punching through Marc's brain. As far as my metaphorical reading is concerned, Lemire and Smallwood explode the feasibility of the assumed superhero work/life balance and needless cycles of violence.

Moon Knight embraces his madness, and as a result, rejects Khonshu's claim on his life post-resurrection. Similarly, the worker's discontent is not the fault of the worker, but the result of their disempowered condition. To paraphrase Franco "Bifo" Berardi,[30] why are workers valuing their work as the most interesting aspect of their lives and willing to increase their time working instead of living a life?

Why in turn, should the employer be credited with granting us a life, represented in Lemire and Smallwood's *Moon Knight* series by the sadism of Khonshu, rabbiting on in Marc's ear and making unreasonable demands on both his physical and mental health?

Economics, statecraft, capitalist growth and globalisation all claim to represent a rational system. However, increasingly, as we look at the world outside our window, as Stan Lee urged us to, it becomes obvious these systems of control are utterly mad.

From man-made climate change to the spread of a global plague due to an unwillingness to deprivatise vaccines. The rising tide of fascism seizing on widespread disenfranchisement to liberal culture wars increasing harm to Trans and queer youths. In the world of Marvel comics, where people are flying through the sky, climbing walls, and giant space gods, Moon Knight's sane costumed peers refuse to change the world that is constantly on the brink of disaster, instead supporting the status quo of the society that cannot deal with these threats in perpetuity. Of course, Marc is mad, he has every reason to be. And perhaps so do we.

---

[30] Who memorably remarked "Capitalism is becoming schizo" (*The Soul at Work*, The MIT Press, 2009).

A Place of Melancholy Comfort: Understanding the Social Issues Portrayed in Doug Moench's Moon Knight

by Jason Kahler

Moon Knight was first truly defined by his creator, writer Doug Moench, with issue one of his first self-titled series. While his first appearances established his look and some details of his M.O., other background details were abandoned in favour of the specifics with which we usually associate the character: the multiple identities, the connection to the Egyptian god Khonshu, and the complicated psychological elements of the characters. Other writers would explore these aspects of Moon Knight's characterization to one degree or another, but none would approach the character's placement within the Marvel Universe, and its society writ large, in the same way as Moench.

Moench embedded the character's complex relationships with the forces he represents deeply into Moon Knight's history. From the character's earliest appearances in his own books, he was positioned to straddle social and cultural identities. Moon Knight was a former-military mercenary. Moon Knight was a wealthy financier. Moon Knight was a streetwise taxi driver. Moon Knight was the templar of an unreliable god. While alternate, and even contradictory, identities have long been a staple of superhero privacy strategies (Clark Kent isn't just Superman in glasses: he's meek, bumbling, passive), Moon Knight's competing identities represent more cross-cultural concerns. Moon Knight's identities aren't just a mask (for example, "Bruce Wayne" is just a mask for Batman, the character's true self), Moon Knight lives within these lives and therefore represents an array of contrasting social and political philosophies. Moon Knight reads as several concerns, in ways that other characters do not.

This essay argues that Moon Knight's position within two movements, *Nationalism* and *Populism*, grants the opportunity to tell stories that weren't being told in other contemporaneous books, especially at Moon Knight's publisher, Marvel Comics. The complications that come from Moon Knight's extra identities are deliberately baked into the character. This allowed Moench to explore elements of culture and society traditional superhero books had yet to make space for. To illustrate Moon Knight's uniqueness to early-80s comic books, this essay discusses two noteworthy "one-shot" stories from the time, "Stained Glass Scarlet" and "Hit It!" from *Moon Knight* issues #14 and #26, respectively. Viewing Moon Knight through this Cultural Criticism lens produces a deeper understanding of what was happening in his comics at this time, especially compared to other books across the genre.

Moon Knight in the Frameworks of Nationalism and Populism

From the late 70s and into the 80s, Marvel books were beginning to look beyond their panels to comment on the world around them. Marvel's comics were always more rooted in real-world problems than their counterparts. The Fantastic Four experienced the typical conflicts of any family, and Peter Parker was always scrambling for money. As the 70s gave way to the 80s, many of Marvel's titles took this worldliness even further. Their heroes often took active roles in the politics and social concerns of the day. This development came in part as a result of a batch of new creators, who were taking over titles in a second wave of talent, that began as the original company guard transitioned to new roles (like Stan Lee) or left the company entirely (like Jack Kirby). They brought new interests and new sensibilities, and these were reflected in their books.

Considering Moon Knight, most modern criticism of the character has been focused on his mental health and the ways in which his Dissociative Identity Disorder has been depicted. These investigations are informed by modern mental health theories and the abilities of comic books to discuss more complicated concepts in the context of superhero stories.[1] Moench was choosing to unpack complicated concepts in his early Moon Knight stories but with a focus on social concerns and the failings of the American social safety net rather than his character's mental health. The landscape of superhero comics was changing in the late 70s and early 80s, as comic book scholars have noted.

Two unique hero types began to emerge at this time and have since been described by comic book researchers. Jason Dittmer's book *Captain America and the Nationalist Superhero: Metaphors, Narratives, and Geopolitics* investigates how certain heroes embody specific nation-states. Whereas *Working-Class Comic Book Heroes: Class Conflict and Populist Politics in Comics*, edited by Marc DiPaolo, turns attention to heroes that are more associated with the people of those nation-states. It's helpful to spend some time thinking through these Nationalist and Populist superheroes before returning to Moon Knight specifically.

As Dittmer explains, Captain America was conceived to embody a certain sense of Americanism. In his first appearance, on the cover of *Captain America Comics* #1 (1940), Cap famously punches Adolf Hitler, effectively entering the war before the United States. His uniquely American machismo is on full display throughout that series and remains when he returns to join the Avengers in *Avengers* #4 (1964). Cap represents the honour and fighting spirit Americans clung to during World War II and later, once he's freed from the ice that preserved him. In Cap, we recognize notions of American exceptionalism, a level of worldwide Manifest Destiny, an image that's aspirational at its best and jingoistic at its worst. While it's true that Cap's symbolism was explored and critiqued during the 1980s, especially during writer Mark Gruenwald's run on the character, these stories often put Cap's nationalistic origins in conflict with what he knew was right and wrong. This served to highlight Cap's foundational

---

[1] Christie, Charlie. "Sane Superheroes: Mental Distress in the Gutters of Moon Knight." *Uncanny Bodies: Superhero Comics and Disability*, ed. Scott Smith and Alaniz José. Pennsylvania State University Press, 2019. Pages 59-78.

nationalism and the role the character played (in-story and in the real world) in how people imagined *American values*.

On the other end of the spectrum are Populist superheroes. Through characters living outside traditional systems of power, creators comment on issues of class and economics. In her chapter in *Working-Class Comic Book Heroes*, "From the Streets to the Swamp: Luke Cage, Man-Thing, and the 1970s Class Issues of Marvel Comics," Blair Davis explores the populism and class structures embodied by Luke Cage, who comes from a lower socio-economic class, and Man-Thing, who, as a muck monster living in the Everglades, is classless.[2] While Davis points out that Marvel books often discussed class issues, Luke Cage and Man-Thing are examples of characters with primarily populist concerns. Characters like Spider-Man, Iron Man, and The Thing are heavily influenced by economics and class but are much more likely to be undertaking typical superheroic activities than Cage or Man-Thing. In their adventures, Cage and Man-Thing specifically lift populist causes and address social concerns like fair housing, drug addiction rehabilitation, and environmental justice.

In Moon Knight, we find a character at the intersection of nationalism and populism. During his early career as a Marine and CIA operative, Moon Knight (in his Marc Spector identity) participates in nationalist, though largely covert, operations that find him questioning his role in the military/political machine much like Captain America does in the 80s. In the opening pages of the character-defining first issue of *Moon Knight* (1980), Spector slaughters local villagers at the behest of his unit leader, the terrorist-for-hire, Roaul Bushman. After the smoke clears and Bushman exults in the easy victory, Spector is more contemplative. "Maybe I'm remembering I'm a professional soldier," he says, "not a butcher!" He's not ready to commit to such depth and introspection, however. Not yet. "Or maybe it's just the heat," Spector says[3]. In this retelling of Moon Knight's origin, Moench positions Spector within the mechanisms of nationalism and the dark underbelly of the military-industrial complex. He's a

---

[2] Davis, Blair. "From the Streets to the Swamp: Luke Cage, Man-Thing, and the 1970s Class Issues of Marvel Comics." *Working-Class Comic Book Heroes: Class Conflict and Populist Politics in Comics*. University Press of Mississippi, 2018. Pages 149-168.

[3] "The Macabre Moon Knight." *Moon Knight* Vol. 1 #1 (1980). By Doug Moench, Bill Sienkiewicz, and B. Sharen.

soldier, having moved on to using his training elsewhere. He maintains some of his nationalist mindset and code, but circumstances are complicating his self-image. It's that complication that will later lead him to become Moon Knight, which is only possible through his nationalist foundations.

As cab driver Jake Lockley, the character moves within more typically populist circles. Later in the same issue, as Lockley, Moon Knight uses his street-level connections to get help in tracking down Bushman's current whereabouts. This is a world, home to Gena's Diner, far removed from the nationalist battlefield that birthed Moon Knight. Moreover, they are separate from the circles the character travels in when assuming his millionaire playboy persona, Steven Grant. Other scholars have taken up the project of unpacking Moon Knight's mental health and the comics' approach to his multiple personalities/dissociative identity disorder, including in this book, so there's no need to travel that road here. What's interesting for considering where Moon Knight is positioned within the broader scheme of Marvel's books, however, is that even at this early stage, Moench was working with the multi-intersectionality of Moon Knight's various identities and putting their contrasting virtues to work for the sake of the story.

These intentional contradictions make Moon Knight unique among his comic book contemporaries. While some characters may have started as nationalist or populist, only to transition into something new as time went on, Moon Knight was, very early, a complex blend of both sets of concerns. Moon Knight's multiple identities don't play a role in his first appearances across *Werewolf by Night* #32-33, they are introduced in his *Marvel Spotlight* story published in 1976.[4] While they make him unique even then, Moench doesn't have the space to explore them deeply until the character's solo series. Once he became something more than the adversary-of-the-month in *Werewolf by Night*, the character was allowed to speak to a more complicated set of ideas. Thinking about the character this way reveals that Moench was playing a different game than most of the other Marvel writers of the time. We can see this with a deeper dive into other titles on the newsstand around the time of Moon Knight's emergence as a character in his own title.

---

[4] "The Crushing Conquer-Lord!" *Marvel Spotlight* Vol. 1 #28 (1976). By Doug Moench, Don Perlin, and I Vartanoff.

Moon Knight: Avatar for Social Conscience

To understand how unique Moon Knight is in the history of Marvel Comics, it's important to view his books alongside the others of the time. Investigating each issue throughout his history would be overly time-consuming. It's productive, however, to contextualize two of Moon Knight's most-appreciated stories, "Stained Glass Scarlett" and "Hit It!" By viewing these two stories in light of what else was on the shelf at the time, we can gain a better picture of Moench's overall intention with the *Moon Knight* book.

In general, these stories may strike modern comic book readers as strange. Moench was writing at a time when the caption was king, the voice of the omniscient narrator peeking behind the curtains of the character's mind. Chris Claremont, writer of *Uncanny X-Men* during this time, was experimenting with using captions as the character's inner voice, eschewing thought balloons, which is a practice in use across a large swathe of comics today. But Moench was still writing captions offering the exposition that grounded readers in the situations. Moreover, Moench was pushing the limits of language in his captions. Not in the sense of using curse words, but elevating language, writing literary captions that move beyond merely setting the stage or offering "Meanwhile, back at the Hall of Justice."

While this chapter is primarily focused on how Moench develops Moon Knight into something comics hadn't quite seen before, his partners in the endeavour deserve a great deal of credit. In particular, artist Bill Sienkiewicz's work on Moon Knight, and later *New Mutants*, has firmly entrenched him as one of the modern masters of the medium. His moody ink work and convention-defying/defining panel layouts lean into Moench's dark subject matter while at the same time allowing Moon Knight to be, when necessary, a comic book superhero. Both "Stained Glass Scarlet" and "Hit it!" benefit greatly from colourist Christie Scheele's decisions. Without the specifics of the visuals in these stories, toying and expanding upon comic book conventions, they would certainly be far less memorable.

"Stained Glass Scarlet," from *Moon Knight* #14,[5] sports a film noir cover featuring a smoking gun in the hands of a femme fatale, and Moon Knight shot

---

[5] "Stained Glass Scarlet." *Moon Knight* Vol. 1 #14 (1981). By Doug Moench, Bill Sienkiewicz, and Christie Scheele.

and crumpled on the ground. The story, however, portrays the woman much more favourably.

The Scarlet from the title is Scarlet Fasinera, and she tells her story to Moon Knight via flashbacks. She's mother to Joe "Mad Dog" Fasinera, a recent prison escapee who's now leaving a trail of mayhem as he cuts loose with his crew. Fasinera's father was a low-level mobster who came to the church where Scarlet was a nun. She sees something in him, they fall in love, and she leaves the sisterhood. Though Scarlet tries to lead her husband down the right path, he remains committed to crime, even after the birth of their son. He's eventually killed by police during a robbery, and Mad Dog decides to start his own life of crime. Scarlet moves into the church, now abandoned, where she met her husband.

Moon Knight deduces Mad Dog is heading to that same church, and they both confront Scarlet. After the ensuing fistfight, Mad Dog shoots Moon Knight. Scarlet and Mad Dog then have a stand-off, guns pointed at each other. Scarlet fires in her son's direction. A warning shot? Poor aim? It's hard to know. However, her intentions are made clear once Mad Dog confirms that he's never going to back down from his life of mayhem: Scarlet fatally shoots her son. As Scarlet slinks away sadly into the night, Moon Knight stands over Mad Dog's body and says one thing: "Guns."[6]

Stained Glass Scarlet, the character, would make some smaller appearances in later books[7] with the addition of some ill-defined psychic connection to Moon Knight. This first appearance, however, pairs comic book drama with social commentary, an important distinction from most of the other books being published at the time. Moench is using the superhero merely as a way for entering the story. Without Moon Knight, the narrative would remain largely unchanged, but Moon Knight's presence is what brings us there. Moench uses the trappings of the superhero story to lure our eyes and direct our gaze. Then he can unravel a story of domestic tragedy and an abandoned woman. More important, however, is the fact that Stained Glass Scarlet recovers her agency after her self-imposed isolation.

---

[6] Ibid.

[7] Notably in *Moon Knight* Vol. 1 #24 (1982) and *Marc Spector: Moon Knight* Vol. 1 #26-31 (1991).

The last page of *Moon Knight* Vol. 1 #14 (1980).

Superhero comic books have a troubled history with how they've handled women. In the medium's earliest days, women were decorative objects or used for lessons about the dangers of hysterics and *womanly emotions*. Comics of the 60s are riddled with examples of women being mistreated, or not treated at all. Strong women began to emerge in the 70s, often stereotyped as the tough, don't-take-any-flack lady. In Stained Glass Starlet, Moench creates a character that bridges the space into the 80s. The move takes place within the context of this short narrative. Scarlet has been cast aside, barely a fixture in her own story, living an existence permanently on pause. Like her early comic counterparts, her life is defined in relation to the men in her life, or more to the point, by the rules the men have established for her to live by. Her breaking into the abandoned church is the first indication that there's a shift occurring in how she will view herself going forward. Killing her son, thereby saving her life, Moon Knight's, and countless others, is the final act of a woman who used to be someone else.

The Stained Glass Scarlet character would go on to make limited appearances after this. In the comics now, the character has died but exists as a paranormal phenomenon sustained by people telling stories about her.[8] "Stained Glass Scarlet," as we'll see, is unique among Marvel's books at the time, but Moench's approach here, of using a superhero to attract attention to a cultural issue, is one he'll continue to use. He returns to this technique with "Hit It!"[9]

On the stands on August 31st, 1982, *Moon Knight* #26 opens with a letter from editor Denny O'Neil. O'Neil lets the reader know that *Moon Knight* is trying to push the boundaries of what a superhero book can do. "(H)ow many liberties can we take with the traditional comic book format?" he asks. It's a valid question, given the story that begins this issue.

"Hit It!" shares the book with another story but leaves an impression well beyond its length. It reads like a poem or the jazz groove it references:

> First there is black.
> Then there is light, and all the colours of jazz.
> And there is sound in these colours.
> A wailing trumpet drips cool violet, threaded with smoke.
> Heavy blue lumbers from the bass...
> ...While the clarinet tantalizes in hot pink counterpoint.
> But the drum...
> The drum beats bright red.

The narrative weaves through this linguistic riffing, eventually revealing a Moon Knight swinging from the rooftops on patrol, and a man, Joe, suffering from a breakdown after reading the obituary of his abusive father.

Comics are always about the interplay and juxtapositions of narrative, words, and art, but "Hit It!" is a lesson in taking advantage of everything a comic book can do. Sienkiewicz's visuals lean into the abstract power of art to use the repeated image of a child's drawing (the sort a child would create when processing physical abuse) to represent the intersection of anguish, memory, and emotional trauma. Joe recalls beatings at the hands of his father. Instead of through a traditional flashback, Sienkiewicz lets the crude crayon drawing

---

[8] "Scarlet." *Moon Knight* Vol. 10 #8 (2022). By Jed Mackay, Alessandro Cappuccio, and Rachelle Rosenburg.
[9] "Hit It!" *Moon Knight* Vol. 1 #26 (1982). By Doug Moench, Bill Sienkiewicz, and Christie Scheele.

represent the details of the child's abuse. It's Hitchcockian: Sienkiewicz knows there's nothing he can show us as terrible as what we can imagine.

Lashing out through memory and rage, Joe begins hitting everyone he encounters, running from place to place, punching people out cold. "He... he *hit* me... for no reason... just *hit* me," says one of Joe's victims.[10] In one particularly jarring sequence, Joe barges into the funeral parlour where his father's coffin waits for the service. Joe bursts through the door and is confronted by a priest. Without a word or explanation, Joe punches the priest squarely in the face.

Moon Knight enters the room and confronts Joe, who reveals his abusive past. Joe implores Moon Knight to hit him, to continue the cycle of violence. Even the priest, holding his face, begs Moon Knight to intervene with a physical response. "Hit me... please hit me..." Joe begs. But Moon Knight remains firm. "No..." he says to the priest. "There's been enough hitting tonight. I won't add to it".[11]

Joe stands and lunges, punching Moon Knight in the back of the head with a *HWAKK*.

In lesser creators' hands, this is the point where Moon Knight would use words, or some soft restraint to subdue Joe, who's clearly struggling, as represented by the thin panels twitching between the present confrontation and the child's drawing. This story, however, is something more. The panels each hit with the impact of a snare drum shot. Beat after beat. "It's too late, Moon Knight," Joe yells. "Nothing can stop it now. So, either hit me or –". And that's what Moon Knight does. A left cross, followed by a right, and then Moon Knight lifts Joe into the air as the caption implores "No, Moon Knight! No! No!" But the decision is made, and Moon Knight clobbers Joe. The star of the book, the hero, leaves Joe, bloody and beaten, on the funeral parlour floor. In the panels depicting the final punches and a frustrated Moon Knight's departure, the captions connect to the music from the story's opening: "And, once started, the drum beats blood... forever."[12]

We are to understand that Moon Knight is frustrated that he was drawn into the never-ending cycle of violence because as the story concludes, he punches a wall. He knows, as the hero, he was supposed to do better, supposed

---

[10] Ibid.
[11] Ibid.
[12] Ibid.

to be better. His first inclinations were correct; we shouldn't perpetuate needless violence, especially when alternatives are clearly available. The ability to commit violence and use physical force may appear like it takes preparation and training, but often, it's the easiest response to a challenging situation.

Comic book heroes use violence as if it's commonplace, and Moon Knight is no different. Even heroes who are typically viewed as portraying high moral standards (like Superman or Captain America) understand that some problems are best solved with a smart left hook.

Stories depicting the hero going in a different direction garner attention. Quiet moments when the violence takes a break often become some of a series' best-remembered stories. Moench and Sienkiewicz go in a different direction, however, and that's what makes this story noteworthy. Instead of making their hero some unassailable paragon of virtue, Moon Knight is shown to be just as vulnerable to being swept up in the cycle of violence as we are. Whether we understand Moon Knight's physical response to Joe to be a decision made out of retribution for being punched from behind or out of acquiescence to the idea that only violence can end violence, the story doesn't end the way these usually do. Comic book heroes rarely get physical with *regular Joes*, that Moon Knight does here speaks to exactly what O'Neil was considering in the issue's opening letter. *Moon Knight* is *not* a traditional comic book.

A large part of the mythos of Moon Knight is his position as the avatar of Khonshu. A lot has already been said in modern critiques of Moon Knight about his relationship with the difficult Egyptian god he worships (or at least works for). Even within the stories themselves, Khonshu's presence, and mere existence, can be called into question. When coupled with his Dissociative Identity Disorder, it complicates just who Moon Knight is as an agent in his own world. These two stories complicate his position even further. Just who is this Moon Knight, and how are we supposed to understand his presence in these stories? While Moon Knight as a character has origins (and in some cases through the years superpowers) from his connection to Khonshu, he remains largely an everyman who glides through multiple worlds. In this way, he is the avatar of the reader as well.

Both "Stained Glass Scarlet" and "Hit It!" present stories that are unexpected within the context of a superhero comic, so readers are immediately placed on unsteady ground. This is not what we expect. In these issues, the make-believe world is not the usual make-believe world of comic books; in fact, it's much closer to *our* world than our comfort prefers. Moon Knight is uncomfortable here, too. He even looks out of place: the only *costume* in panels full of civilians, regular people with (mostly) regular problems in little need of a superhero. Since there are no superheroes needed, Moon Knight can be our eyes and ears. These stories get told because he is there.

Comic books draw our imaginations into their stories because we can see ourselves flying through the air, lifting cars, or climbing along the wall like a spider. In these issues, we see ourselves just there, bearing witness and experiencing the emotions through which Moon Knight progresses. "Stained Glass Starlet" and "Hit It!" each cast a bright light on societal ills. That's special for their time. The stories avoid the easy answers, however. The hero cannot stop domestic abuse, he cannot come between a man's criminal destruction if the man does not wish to change. Moon Knight, like the reader he represents in these stories, is powerless against such fundamental and systemic flaws in our systems. For everything he can do, he can't turn back time, and he can't stop someone hellbent on poor decisions. He gives voice to readers' frustrations in the closing moments of each story, with the punching of the wall in "Hit it!" and the regretful moment he spares to consider Mad Dog's gun.

Moon Knight is positioned between the competing philosophies of nationalism and populism. He's dedicated to the ideals of socialism, but also tethered to the nationalistic urge to impose a societal norm. His position is confined by and beholden to their very structures. Empowered and restrained by each sensibility.

Considering the Neighbourhood: Moon Knight's Contemporaries

Depending on how you want to count them, Marvel Comics published about 25 books with the cover date of December 1981.[13] Marvel also published several books not directly connected to the shared universe of their main line at the time. A cursory look through that month's offerings reveals that *Moon Knight* was indeed a book like few others at the time, addressing issues and unpeeling what it means to be a hero in ways the other titles weren't considering. Most of the books bearing that cover date are typical superhero fare.

---

[13] Marvel Fandom, December 1981.
marvel.fandom.com/wiki/Category:Comics_Released_in_December,_1981

For example, *The Amazing Spider-Man* #223 features Spidey squaring off against the Red Ghost and his apes. It's a mad scientist story. Perhaps it's a little noteworthy because the Red Ghost isn't usually a Spider-Man villain, but Spidey's met his share of crazy scientists throughout his history. In *Fantastic Four* #237, the team faces off against a villain of the month, Spinnerette. The overall issue features the FF's usual hallmark family drama. *Avengers* #214 continues the drama with the psychological challenges encountered by Hank Pym. Recent issues see Pym expelled from The Avengers over the way he treats his wife, The Wasp, Janet Van Dyne. While this storyline forms the basis of a lot of Pym's later character development, looking at the issue at the moment, it doesn't break any of the norms for superhero team books. *Uncanny X-Men* #152, not too far removed from the groundbreaking "Days of Future Past" storyline, is another typical issue, continuing the increased importance of Kitty Pride within the series.

Not every December 1981 title was as typical as the others, however. That month's *Captain America*, from writer J. M. DeMatteis and penciler Mike Zeck, interestingly tells a different type of story than most of its contemporaries. In issue #264's story "American Dreamers," Cap finds himself in a series of alternate worlds built from the imaginations of racists and Nazi sympathizers. The book still retains many of the trappings of typical comics: evil masterminds and the fantastical Telepathy Augmentor. The difference is DeMatteis' story explores the potential impact of hatred and fascist ideology, which is a much deeper message than the average villain of the month smash-up. *Captain America* would continue to be a title unafraid to question and explore politics throughout the 80s, notably during the long run of writer Mark Gruenwald.

Another book that offers an interesting comparison is issue #177 of *Daredevil*, written and drawn by Frank Miller, with important contributions by Klaus Jenson on inks. The issue takes the opportunity to advance several subplots while Daredevil tries to restart his lost radar sense. He finds his mentor, Stick, who puts Daredevil through a series of challenges designed to force him to confront the demons of his past. The demons become literal in one of a series of dream sequences where Daredevil faces off against the actual Devil, drawn by Miller as a goat/spider hybrid with an exposed spine. The story is a hallucinogenic trip. Though they've had few interactions within comics, Daredevil and Moon Knight have often been similar characters: street-level heroes without the advantage of superhuman strength, slight assistance from technology but mostly relying on skill, mental and emotional torment and anguish, important runs of stories defined by *auteur*-level writers and artists. There's more to be said about the connection between these two characters, and it's not surprising that the approaches to storytelling employed by both books are contrary to the average output of the time.

Even among these books that explore new storytelling grounds, *Moon Knight* of this time (the month in which "Stained Glass Scarlet" arrived on newsstands) stands out from the crowd. *Daredevil* may be gritty, and *Captain America* may be working to address cultural issues, but *Moon Knight* makes the superheroics tangential to the overall story. Taking an even sharper view and inspecting the Marvel Comics published the same week as "Hit It!" reveals the continuing trend.

Marvel released "Hit It!" the same day the company released the following books:

Amazing Spider-Man Annual #16
Amazing Spider-Man #235
Avengers Annual #11
Doctor Strange Vol. 2 #56
Micronauts #48
Wolverine #4 (last issue of a limited series)[14]

This is an interesting week for comic book pop culture history, though in the context of this discussion, it supports the overall thesis of *Moon Knight*'s uniqueness at the time. The only book that takes risks, story-wise, is the final issue of Wolverine's limited series. Across the series, Wolverine is shown to be working out the competing impulses of his human and his animal instincts. He is positioned as a sort of modern samurai. He's also clearly a killer, which sets him apart from the overwhelming majority of heroes, especially at this time. This limited series forms the basis of much of Wolverine's characterization for many years afterwards and is considered by many to be the definitive Wolverine story.

Amazing Spider-Man Annual #16 features the first appearance of Monica Rambeau, the second Captain Marvel. The introduction of a powerful, female, African American superhero is noteworthy. While the story itself is fairly boilerplate, Rambeau goes on to play an interesting role in the Marvel Universe,

[14] Marvel Fandom, week 35 1982.
marvel.fandom.com/wiki/Category:Week_35,_1982

disappearing from books for long stretches at times, but also leading the Avengers and going through a string of different codenames. Her presence in the Marvel Cinematic Universe has created more interest in the character, especially recently, and she's been promoted to joining the Thunderbolts in the series' 2022 reboot. (Given the history of baits-and-switches with the Thunderbolts, there are no guarantees that the promotions are truthful, but they seem to be as of this writing.)

Both of those issues continue to be sought-after by collectors for the characters and the importance they've had in media beyond comics. However, it's "Hit It!" which distinguishes itself thematically and artistically. It pushes the boundaries of the kind of stories superhero comics could tell, and the ways those stories could be told. Again, Moench is playing a very different game in his books than we see in Marvel's offerings in general, and these stories would pave the way for more socially conscious stories to make their way into mainstream superhero comics.

"A Place of Melancholy Comfort"

On the second page of "Stained Glass Scarlet," Moench describes the abandoned church that she's adopted as her refuge/hiding place: "But high above the corruption, just under the church's vaulted roof in what was once the attic, there is a place of melancholy comfort... if not sanctuary."[15] That turn of phrase might well be describing Moench's early *Moon Knight* stories for us in general. These stories do not end happily. They do not leave us feeling good. Rather, we share in Moon Knight's frustrations and defeatism. The crumbling or ineffective social safety net offers little hope, especially for those of us who struggle in the dark.

If we can't take sanctuary, then, there is comfort in knowing that these stories, which tell of the trials experienced by those without capes or superpowers, are worthy of notice. Worthy of being told. And that if they're being told, there's at least a chance we'll attract, or become, heroes of our own.

---

[15] "Stained Glass Scarlet." *Moon Knight* Vol. 1 #14 (1981). By Doug Moench, Bill Sienkiewicz, and Christie Scheele.

Exploring a Mindscape

by Tony Farina

On the cover of issue #1 of Jeff Lemire, Greg Smallwood, and Jordie Bellaire's Moon Knight run, readers are confronted by Smallwood's brilliant art, our titular hero in a straitjacket staring back at the reader. It is a bit disconcerting, to say the least, but it is also the opening salvo of a run that forces readers to be uncomfortable and question what they think they know.

Readers come to comics aware of the formula. They understand. It is welcoming. It makes sense. There is some clarity to this. These 14 issues of Moon Knight upend all of this on every level. The off-kilter world of the first few pages is a dream, but the reality of the situation is much worse. Marc is in a hospital. It is specifically called an insane asylum. Lemire wants readers to know that this isn't a place for healing, it is a place to be held captive. The distinction is important. The collected edition cover has the word *Lunatic* on it, hammering home the intent. Lemire wants the readers to know that everything they are about to see is done on purpose. Every word, every line, and every colour choice are part of a bigger story, all part of a bigger commentary on how we treat the mentally ill both in art and in the world. He makes comparisons to things the reader understands and knows while asking the reader to analyze those same things through a new lens.

For Lemire to pull this off, he first makes the reader see things differently. He forcibly adjusts the reader's perspective. He does this by taking everything conventional about the art form and flipping it sideways. In years past, characters said their inside thoughts outside. Spider-man was often seen telling

The cover to *Moon Knight* Vol. 8 #1 (2016).

anyone who would listen his whole plan. Every baddie in the Marvel Universe could have been confused with exposition as he (it was almost always a he) did his dastardly deeds. Stan Lee did this in an effort to help the readers along. Eventually, in the hands of other writers, it was acceptable for characters to have a running monologue in square dialogue boxes informing the reader that these were the inner thoughts not being said aloud. The reader was privy to the inner thoughts of the character.

Lemire never does this once in this entire run. This is a bold move. Asking readers to reframe what they know about the form in an independent comic is one thing, asking them to disregard years of standard practice in a Marvel comic is something else. It is risky, yet it makes perfect sense for the story he wants to tell. Also, Lemire need not worry because Smallwood, Bellaire (and the guest artists in later issues), provide everything the reader needs.

Bobby and Billy, the two evil guards/orderlies, are drawn quite differently. One of them is a white, blonde man with glasses and a moustache, the other is an African American man with an afro, complete with an embedded pick. Both characters look like they came out of a 1970s exploitation film. They seem familiar to the reader because these stereotypical images have been used over and over. So, while they look different, they are as indistinguishable as Rosencrantz and Guildenstern are in *Hamlet*. It is here that readers more deeply understand what it is Lemire is doing. He is presenting them with something they understand, movie bad guys with little to no motivation but to be bullies to our hero, while commenting on their willingness to harm someone, whom an authority figure has deemed to be mentally unwell. Billy and Bobby are there to please. They are blunt instruments, and they don't care. They may be following the orders of Dr Emmet, but they enjoy the work. Hurting Marc is joyous for them just as tricking Hamlet is seen as an adventure to Rosencrantz and Guildenstern. We see it in the panels when they shock him. In the panels where they beat him. In the panels where they threaten him. There is always a knowing look between them and Marc. They are evil. They don't care if Marc knows which of them is Billy and which one of them is Bobby as long as he knows that they are going to hurt him, and they are going to enjoy it.

If the eyes are the windows to the soul Billy and Bobby's clear-eyed focus, shows readers everything in comparison to the rest of the cast in the first four issues. Readers see the drugged-out look of the patients. They stare blankly into space or at each other without any sense of focus. Lemire doesn't need to write "These people seem out of it" nor does he have to have Marc say, "I feel woozy," either aloud or in a thought bubble. We simply see it. This is all setting us up for the first arrival of Moon Knight. The one shown on the cover of the trade. Marc Spector, with a ripped sheet over his head, twisted into Moon Knight's cowl. The eye holes look as if a child were dressing up as a ghost for Halloween. It is through those crudely cut eye holes that we see, for the first time, Marc Spector's eyes wide open. He knows exactly what he is doing. The haze is gone. We understand that he is fully present for the first time in this whole series. Lemire knows readers understand this because Smallwood shows it. It may not be noticeable during the first read because there is so much going on to keep the reader disoriented but every one of these artistic choices is made to convey a larger message. Like any good storyteller, Lemire shows the readers everything but doesn't put big red arrows over it, explicitly directing the reader. He expects them to come along for the ride. It helps that he has some of the best artists in the business to tell the story he wants to tell.

Case in point; several pages into the story and readers are put off-kilter by blurry, almost dreamlike images. Jordie Bellaire's colours on these first few pages are deliberately hazy. Our hero, Marc Spector, is lost and confused. We are seeing things not from his eyes, but through his state of mind. When he awakes, the images become crystal clear. Bellaire tightens everything up and *reality* crashes down on Spector and the reader. This is a bad place, where bad things happen. Some of it must be real.

Just when the reader may start to re-find their footing and understand who is who, and what is what, Lemire enlists more artists to create a slippery surface. Between issues #5-9, each of Marc's personalities gets their own art style. Wilfredo Torres and Michael Garland take on Steven Grant, Francesco Francavilla draws the Jake Lockley pages and James Stokoe draws the space adventures of The Moon Knight.

Grant's pages are sharp and brightly coloured, like a technicolour film of the 1940s. He is a high-class, well-to-do man about town who works in the film industry. While he is confused as to what is going on, the world around him is not. Steven Grant, unlike Marc Spector, is on full display for all to see. Not one hair is out of place and his white outfit looks freshly pressed and cleaned. These pages form a stark contrast to those the reader has already read, covering the period spent in the hospital.

Jake Lockley finds himself in a surrealist noir painting. He is a creature of the night, a cabbie who ventures into the dark corners of the city and so everything is equal parts obscured and exposed in coloured light. The alleys and the doorways are completely black while the neon lights bathe everyone in purples and pinks. Like Spector, he is a fighter and so his clothes, his face and everything about his world are ratty and worn. He is aware of the hospital, but he doesn't want to go. However, unlike Grant, who must be spurred into action, Lockley is born ready.

There is a glaring difference within the pages that feature Grant, making the Moon Knight movie and the actual movie. In the Grant pages, it looks like a movie set. The props look fake. The costumes fit badly. It looks like a movie set, with a dropped boom mic in one panel for full effect. There is something *real* about Grant's life. Compared to the other stories, Grant's world seems to be *the* world where the readers live. Yet there are moments when the reader is presented with what would be on screen and given glimpses of a world within a world. The cheapness falls away and it looks like an adventure.

However, when readers are thrown into the final Moon Knight world Marc Spector reappears as a space ace fighting the Space Wolves. The images Stokoe creates are cartoonish and exaggerated on purpose. While we as the reader, know this is fiction, a comic, the vast difference in style and context between the worlds provides a distance from what is identified as the norm, the *real*, for the reader. The temptation of the *real* in Grant's world compared to the ludicrousness of the other worlds. The reader has an omnipotent view, able to see these shifts in reality, while Marc does not.

For two more issues, readers feel exactly what it is like for Marc Spector, Jake Lockley, and Steven Grant to share one body. The disorientation is complete. The reader has succumbed to the fact that nothing they thought they knew was real. They feel slightly off and unsure of themselves, just like Marc. The artists, sometimes subtly and sometimes overtly, connect these stories while constantly reminding us that Marc is on the run from Billy and Bobby, who like Rosencrantz and Guildenstern are trying to capture a seemingly mad prince.

Billy and Bobby use words like crazy, sick, and insane while Spector is beaten, and injected with some kind of drug against his will. This makes the reader wonder if all of this is real or a product of the drugs. What world is the real world? It is only upon the appearance of Mr Knight, the calm, regal, totally self-assured personality that readers see any semblance of normality. Even then, when he has his mask on, he is Mr Knight, and when it is off, he is Marc Spector. Again, whatever we think we know, we don't know. When Mr Knight appears, even though we don't see his face, we see through the body language, drawn by Smallwood, that Mr Knight is self-assured, clear-headed, and in charge. Moreover, Lemire's choice of using the Mr Knight name is also important. In the mental institution, Marc Spector is called Marc by his fellow patients and Dr Emmet. The guards, when not using pejoratives, call him Spector. Grant, Lockley, and the space version of Marc are all called all kinds of names.

This is the moment Lemire, and company reconnect with the readers and ask them to feel empathy for all the personalities before they enter into the third act. The creators have put the readers through a lot. They have asked the readers to examine themselves. How have they behaved? To whom do they most relate? Are they a Spector, a Grant, or a Lockley? Are they Mr Knight or are they Moon Knight? Or worse, are they Bobby or Billy? What would they do if they met one of these people on the street, at work, or across the table during a family dinner? What do they think about people with mental illnesses? What do they really know?

Lemire and company remind readers that everyone, at some point, has called someone or something *crazy*. Hundreds of pejorative synonyms of the word crazy are bandied about in seemingly polite society. Sometimes, those words have flipped meanings to be used as a positive. Athletes who are *in the zone* are often referred to as being *out of their minds* and someone who completes an extreme feat could be called *insane* but in a good way. However, in those specific instances, those words are understood in context as either ironic, hyperbolic, or sometimes both. It is not, however, in those instances ever used negatively. Yet, when directed at people who have a mental illness or who have a learning disability, the words are used only negatively and aggressively.

There is a children's saying, "Sticks and stones may break my bones, but words will never hurt me." There are several takes on the exact phraseology, but in the end, the idea is that physical violence is exponentially worse than verbal abuse. That is true in the immediate. One would rather be called an epithet than punched in the nose. However, the nose will heal. Even if in the moment it looks (and feels) bad, in the long run, a punch in the nose might be nothing more than a funny story one can share over cocktails later in life. One may even be able to learn something from the interaction. A punch in the nose may lead to a person taking self-defence classes, or it may be an awakening moment for how to act because maybe, just maybe, the person who was punched in the nose instigated the situation. Maybe a punch in the nose will make someone change their behaviour, for the better. While we can make these speculations, we must understand that this is a silly saying meant to make kids feel better when they are picked on in school.

Conversely, being called something demeaning, while in the moment may seemingly cause no damage, could, and often does carry with it long psychological scars. If a young person of colour is told repeatedly that he is lesser because of his race, he will more than likely go on to feel that he is lesser. If a young woman is told that girls can't do something because girls are less than boys, she may grow up to think that and will perpetuate the patriarchal stereotype. Research shows that verbal abuse, this includes so-called playground bullying, alters the grey matter in the brain creating neural pathways that become permanent if the bullying does not stop. Similarly, adults have shown that mental anguish causes the same pain receptors in the brain to light up as when experiencing physical pain.[1]

The thing is all pain is pain. Physical pain can lead to emotional pain. Emotional pain can cause crippling anxiety as well as other severe levels of psychological distress. This stress can be situational and overcome with therapy, medical help, or both but it can also exacerbate. Both can lead to post-traumatic stress disorder or, in extreme cases, Dissociative Identity Disorder (DID).

DID, as it has been known since 1994, was defined by the developers and creators of the *Diagnostic and Statistical Manual of Mental Disorders* (DSM) but was not always labelled as such. The idea of a person having more than one dissociative personality dates back to the 18th Century. The term used then was "exchanged personalities" making it seem as though there was a host body, seemingly possessed by someone new.[2] In this earliest recorded instance, a young 20-year-old German woman suddenly began speaking with a perfect French accent. The new personality was aware of the host's personality, but the host knew nothing of the other. The study of "exchanged personality"

---

[1] Streep, Peg (reviewed by Jessica Shrader). "5 Things Everyone Must Understand about Verbal Abuse." Psychology Today, 2016. www.psychologytoday.com/us/blog/tech-support/201602/5-things-everyone-must-understand-about-verbal-abuse

[2] Ryder, Gina and Christie Craft (reviewed by Dr Matthew Boland). "The History of Schizophrenia." PsychCentral, 2022. psychcentral.com/schizophrenia/history-of-schizophrenia

continued until the 20th Century when Freud started diagnosing schizophrenia.[3]

However, the disorder did not go unnoticed, and those non-Freudians continued to explore the idea of dissociative personalities. In 1952, the DSM-I created a label for dissociative disorder. A variety of these were studied under a variety of names until 1987 when the DSM-III-R finally cemented the phrase and new diagnosis; "Multiple Personality Disorder", harkening back to the original line of thinking that there was a host body. The term was, for all intents and purposes a reaction to the pop culture phenomenon of the books *Three Faces of Eve*[4] and *Sybil*.[5] Until those books and subsequent movies, the *masses* were mostly unaware that this kind of disorder even existed. Regardless of the veracity of those stories, the idea took hold in the public consciousness and the term stuck around for years.

In 1957, the book and the film *The Three Faces of Eve* burst onto the scene. Written by Corbett H. Thigpen and Hervey M. Cleckley, the book expands the story of Eve White, a patient of theirs who was the subject of a 1954 paper. Twentieth Century Fox bought the rights to the book based on a galley they received and subsequently released the film within a few months of the book's publication. The star of the film, Joanne Woodward won an Academy Award for the film, thus vaulting the book onto the best-seller list. This was the first time the concept of Multiple Personality Disorder had been addressed in such a public way. This film raised awareness of the disorder and kept it in the public eye.[6]

However, as is often the case, the attention span of people wanes. There was no home video and books were, for the most part, read once and put on a shelf. So, in 1973, when *Sybil,* written by Flora Rheta Schrieber was released, a new generation of readers discovered the ideas of what someone with a Multiple Personality could be. Unlike Eve, Sybil was said to have 16 distinct personalities making her case even more intriguing. The book sold over 6 million copies and was made into a 1976 limited-run TV series. Neilson reports

---

[3] Ibid.

[4] Thigpen, Corbett H. and Hervey M. Cleckly. *The Three Faces of Eve*. Secker & Warburg, 1957.

[5] Schreiber, Flora Rheta. *Sybil: The Classic True Story of a Woman Possessed by Sixteen Personalities*. Grand Central Publishing, 1973.

[6] Morris, Susan D. "The Three Faces of Eve." University of Georgia Libraries, 2013. www.georgiaencyclopedia.org/articles/arts-culture/the-three-faces-of-eve/

that one out of every five people in America watched the show. Because it was on TV and able to run again in reruns, *Sybil* became the catalyst for understanding and acceptance of the disorder.

In fact, the book and movie were so influential that they played a part in helping people understand another MPD case in Ohio in 1977. A man named Billy Milligan was found to not be responsible for acts of rape, because he was diagnosed as having 24 separate personalities, and could not be responsible for the actions of the other personalities. This decision was reached, and the court was influenced by public opinion and the response to the book and TV series, *Sybil*.[7] Whether this was the right call is a debate for a different essay.

While the language was once again softened in 1994 with the DSM-IV, many people still think of those who suffer from this affliction as multiples. They consider the disorder something akin to possession, or they think the person with the disorder is a committed huckster putting on a Prestige level act. Of course, no one who makes these claims ever wonders why someone would do that. Why would someone go out of their way to draw that kind of negative attention and name-calling? No one and this phrase is used with tongue firmly planted in cheek here, in their right mind would.

Considering this wider historical context readers must then begin the deep dive into the 14-issue Lemire, Smallwood, and Bellaire run. With all of this background, it can be assumed that the creative team knew exactly what they were doing. In the first few issues, they maintain reader disorientation by keeping Marc disoriented. He hears voices that may or may not be there and he sees things that may also be phantoms. His version of reality is constantly shifting like sand under his feet. He sees sand under his feet that no one else can see, but it is all too real for him.

The trick here is that the readers and the other members of the cast are participating in the same way. The other inhabitants of the hospital act as avatars for the readers. They are unsure of what is going on with Marc because he has been, like so many people who have DID in the real world, mistreated, both literally and figuratively, and misdiagnosed. His *therapist*, whom readers find out has ulterior motives, even goes so far as to say of his journal, "These

---

[7] Smail, Gretchen. "How Sybil Bolstered Billy Milligan's Criminal Case." Bustle, 2021. www.bustle.com/entertainment/the-sybil-book-movie-story-plot-billy-milligan

are just the scribbles of a sick man." To which Marc responds, "No. This is history. These are records. All of this happened. This is my life..."[8]

The easy thing to do here is to go along with this diagnosis. Marc is just a *sick* man. A man who is most likely delusional or schizophrenic, with no supernatural powers, but remembers having powers, and remembers being Marc Spector, Steven Grant, Jake Lockley, as well as several variations of Moon Knight. The reason the reader must believe this to be true is that to believe anything else goes against what we've been told to believe.

The language of *wellness* has dictated and defined what we determine to be a well and sane person. People have one name and one personality. They only see what is there, and they don't hear phantom voices. If they do anything remotely different, they are wrong, they are broken, and they are most assuredly *insane*. It makes processing these differences easier for people to slap a label on the *broken* person. Then apply the worst kind of treatments, to shut them up and make them *better*, or at least be seen to be attempting to make them better.

In the world presented, the world of Moon Knight, that is to say, the Marvel Comic book Universe, Marc Spector is diagnosed as *sick and insane*. However, there is a man who dresses up like a blue and red spider to fight a man in a suit with metallic appendages. There is a woman who, due to a blood transfusion from her cousin, is 8 feet tall, has green, unbreakable skin, fights crime, and cracks wise, all while being a practising attorney. Most egregious is that in New York State, there is a man, who can not only manipulate everyone around him with his mind, but he is also collecting *special* children and turning them into soldiers, one of whom eventually committed full genocide against an alien race. Lemire is well aware that the readers of this book know those things. He forces the reader to grapple with these juxtapositions. He makes them ask themselves if there is a difference between the actions of Marc and all the other vigilante superheroes. Yet, it is a man who is sometimes confused about his name, or his background that is locked in a room, put in a straitjacket, and electrocuted.

The truth is that electroshock therapy seemingly works and that can make it appealing. The troubled individual is juiced within an inch of their life and is unsurprisingly much more tacit. The problem is that it is short-lived. A 2009

---

[8] "Welcome to New Egypt: Part Two." *Moon Knight* Vol. 8 #2 (2016). By Jeff Lemire, Greg Smallwood, and Jordie Bellaire.

study[9] proved that most people, over 80 percent of patients, treated this way relapse within 6 months of treatment. Whereas those who have talk therapy, loving environments, and the proper medication to address the correct diagnosis, have a much more successful recovery and integration into their lives. So, what does that mean for Marc? He is being electrocuted and yet, he is spending time with his alternate personalities. Spector isn't keeping any of this secret from his captors and Lemire isn't keeping it secret from the reader. So, they are forced to ask themselves, why does this happen? Is this worth it? What would happen if people just did the seemingly impossible and believed and accepted Marc?

The journey of Lemire and company's *Moon Knight* series is a commentary on treatment vs. acceptance, and this is where the intersection of language comes in. The story unfolds with Marc taking on the Mr Knight persona. He asks those with him, the other escaped inmates, to call him Mr Knight, and to a person, they do. They know him only as Marc even though Steven and Jake have both made appearances during their stay at the asylum. Yet, when they see him and he asks to be called Mr Knight, they give him the respect he requests. They don't argue with him as the doctors and orderlies do. They don't belittle him. Granted, they are also patients in the world's worst mental hospital. Readers are automatically aware of them but mentally ill doesn't mean stupid. They trust him explicitly and from that trust, Marc begins to heal.

As his hero's journey continues, after he has figured out his allies, Marc must face his supreme ordeal. For someone with DID, that often means looking backwards at the root cause. Of course, this is a comic book, so the obvious answer is that Khonshu is the root cause stemming from the trauma Marc suffers in the Army. That story is all on full display in the text, but what we see, in one of the quieter moments, is much more terrible. In the third act, back in the hands of Smallwood alone, we see all the characters meeting, in the same world, drawn in the same style. This artistic choice stabilizes everything for the reader. They are, like the characters, all on equal footing and the secrets are ready to be revealed.

---

[9] Roher, G. et al. "Relapse rate within 6 months after successful ECT: a naturalistic prospective peer- and self-assessment analysis." PubMed, 2009. pubmed.ncbi.nlm.nih.gov/19703381/

When Marc first meets Steven, he is just a child. People who suffer from DID often discover that the first dissociation happened at a young age, following a traumatic event. Usually, that event is so traumatic that the original personality isn't even aware of the event. That person may or may not ever face it, but the first dissociation is all too aware of exactly what happened. That personality exists as a protector. Without explicitly saying it, Lemire is telling us that something terrible happened to Marc long before he joined the Army.

We are reintroduced to Marc as a teenager, when he returns from the home he's been left in, after Steven's first appearance, for his father's funeral. We find that Jake is now fully in control, helping Marc through the event. Why is he there? Sure, the death of a parent is traumatic, but the full conversation shows something that could be more insidious.

This tale begins with a powerless Marc Spector. He is just a mortal grappling with childhood trauma assisted by his alter personalities. We are then confronted with the idea that Khonshu tells Marc he is his *father*. Lemire deliberately makes the story confusing. Smallwood and Bellaire distort the images intentionally. We are made to ask questions. Should we take things at face value? Is Khonshu the root cause of everything or is Khonshu the manifestation of his actual father, Rabbi Spector? The answer is not clear, but Lemire is asking the reader not to dismiss it out of hand. He asks us to consider the alternative. Maybe Marc Spector is a good man, who suffered horrible childhood trauma at the hands of his father, and he wants to become a hero to stop this from happening to others.

This is a question that springs forth from an idea planted in 1982, in Issue #26 of Moon Knight's first solo comic, "Hit It" written by Doug Moench and drawn by Bill Sienkiewicz. In that issue, readers spend most of their time with a young man, Joe, who, confronted by the death of his abusive father, runs through New York, punching strangers until he arrives at the dead body of his father. Moon Knight follows the carnage and confronts the man who is full of angst and rage over the fact that he can't enact his revenge on his father now that he is dead.

Confronted with the reality of the situation, Moon Knight, feeling a connection to this poor soul, refuses to hit him even at the behest of Joe himself. Yet, when Joe attacks Moon Knight, he too snaps, acting out in the way that hurt little boys act out and he punches and punches Joe until he is bloody and unconscious. Marc walks away angry with himself. The circle of violence was not broken. He says, "And so, Moon Knight, the night was yours after all...And once started, the drum beats blood-red...forever."[10]

So there, we see that Marc has tried and failed. Did that failure all those years ago, push him to create even more personalities that were designed to protect himself, from himself? Are Moon Knight and subsequently Mr Knight just the logical extensions of the life of someone with DID? Is Marc Spector Moon Knight or is Moon Knight just his own person? This text seems to indicate the latter, not the former.

While future stories of Moon Knight will specify and explore the trauma that caused the creation of Steven and Jake, Lemire asks us to wonder if Elias Spector was explicitly to blame, or was he only guilty of covering up for a fellow man of the cloth? It is hard to think otherwise, retrospectively now that *Moon Knight* #194[11] (written by Max Bemis) makes this crystal clear. However, at the time, it seems that Lemire had a different take on the trauma and more importantly how to deal with the trauma in a real, respectful way.

Lemire takes a stand. His run makes it clear that he does not believe that locking someone away who suffers from mental illness is the solution. Tarring people with mental illness with the same brush is not the solution. Each case of clinical depression, obsessive-compulsive disorder, or post-traumatic stress disorder is unique. This is widely understood and yet, DID is still considered in simple terms, through one myopic lens.

A cursory read of this run on *Moon Knight* could be seen in simple terms as just introducing readers to the Moon Knight character, on the backs of artists who are at the top of their game. All these artists are widely considered elite and either worked on or created some groundbreaking series. Marvel's decision to put them in one book was, to use a phrase from another genre, inspired casting. Readers who didn't know the history of Moon Knight may, just by being fans of any one of these talents, throw this series in the pull box because neither Lemire, Smallwood, or Bellaire have ever let anyone down, only to be surprised later by a handful of other talented artists, who further elevated the story. This writer does not doubt that this happened and many of those readers

---

[10] "Hit It." *Moon Knight* Vol. 1 #26 (1982). By Doug Moench, Bill Sienkiewicz, and Christie Scheele.
[11] This issue number occurs after Marvel returned to "legacy numbering" for a short while, so it was *not* the 194th issue.

were thrilled to have a smartly written, expertly drawn, and beautifully coloured series.

However, once readers think about this series through the historical, artistic, linguistic, and psychological lens, this is more than just a way to get new readers to *Moon Knight*. This series is a commentary on the plight and treatment of the mentally ill in general and those with DID in particular. By using the familiar tropes of comic books and classic literature, and making them unfamiliar, this whole series, like the cover of the collected edition, stares right at the readers and dares them to enter this world.

It was a bold decision, and it will have long-lasting societal ramifications in lieu of the fact that many of the images from this run appeared directly in the new Disney Plus series. Just like pop culture changed the way those who suffered severe psychological damage were seen in the 50s and 70s with *Three Faces of Eve* and *Sybil*, *Moon Knight* has the power to change the way people see these people all over again. This time, in a positive light.

Retcons and the Very Model of the Modern Moench Moon Knight

by Brian Cronin

If you had to pick the single most important creator in the history of Moon Knight, it would have to be writer Doug Moench, co-creator of Moon Knight with artist Don Perlin, as an antagonist for Jack Russell, in 1975's *Werewolf by Night* #32. Soon after Moench and Perlin reformulated Moon Knight as a superhero in a solo feature in *Marvel Spotlight* issue #28 (1976). Moench wrote Moon Knight's first regular feature as a recurring backup in *Hulk! Magazine* #11 in 1978 (being paired with artist Bill Sienkiewicz in *Hulk! Magazine* #13) and finally launched Moon Knight's first solo ongoing series alongside Sienkiewicz in 1980. Moench wrote almost every issue of that series before leaving the book in 1983 with issue #33.

The fascinating aspect of Moon Knight's journey through that eight-year period, where Moench was essentially the only writer of Moon Knight,[1] is how Moench used retcons to make changes to the character's status quo and backstory until he finally landed on his *ideal* version of Moon Knight. Moench's

---

[1] David Kraft had Moon Knight briefly join the Defenders in 1977 before the *Hulk! Magazine* feature launched.

use of retcons with Moon Knight is unlike any use of retcons in superhero history.

The term *retroactive continuity*, now better known as a *retcon*, was introduced to the comic world in the letter pages of *All Star Squadron*, Roy Thomas' series set on an alternate version of Earth detailing untold stories during World War II. Fans were interested in how Thomas would write new stories set in the past of some notable heroes while making sure to keep everything straight with the later continuity of the superheroes. When one fan wrote about that topic in *All Star Squadron* #18, Thomas replied, "We like to think that an enthusiastic ALL-STAR booster at one of Adam Malin's Creation Conventions in San Diego came up with the best name for it a few months back: 'Retroactive Continuity.' Has kind of a ring to it, don't you think?"[2]

It did have a nice ring to it, but the shortened term, *retcon* had an even nicer ring to it. In the years since the term has generally evolved from Thomas' original usage, as simply adding to the story of a character through new revelations about their past (like Batman learning in 1948's *Batman* #47 that his parents had been murdered by a criminal named Joe Chill) and is now used to describe new stories that specifically contradict earlier published stories (like the Batman comic book titles in 1994 changing his history so that he never discovered that Joe Chill killed his parents.). It is amusing to note that the term retcon has been essentially *retconned* to mean something different from how Thomas first used it.

One of the reasons retcons played such a major role in Roy Thomas' *All-Star Squadron* work was the looser approach to continuity that DC had taken for several decades. Thus, Thomas was almost playing catch up with *fixing* DC's continuity, when he moved from Marvel to DC in 1980. In the big two, there are two key types of continuity in the world of serialized fiction, the continuity of a specific character/title, and then there is shared continuity. It is almost impossible to avoid the former kind of continuity, even if it is something as simple as continuing to note that Clark Kent and Lois Lane work at the Daily Planet for their editor Perry White (and, of course, even there, that is a retcon, as well, as in the original issues of *Action Comics*, Clark and Lois worked at the Daily Star for their editor, George Taylor). In the early days of comic books, the

---

[2] Thomas, Ray. Letters page. *All-Star Squadron* Vol. 1 #18 (1983).

idea was that the stories being written were disposable. So, when it came to less important details (like, for instance, where did Superman get his cape from?), writers would make up their backstories based on the story at hand. It was only after many years that the Superman titles even began to try to apply some sort of consistency to their continuity.

This approach was how all comic books were created in the early *Golden Age*. For instance, a standard issue of *Action Comics* in 1940 would have seven different ongoing features inside. They would each have their own continuity and nothing in the Zatara feature would impact the Superman or Morgan feature. This way of operating changed for good in May 1940 when MLJ Comics[3] *Pep Comics* #4 had a story starring its patriotic superhero, the Shield, ending with the Shield noting that the story would continue into the Wizard feature in *Top Notch Comics* #5. In November 1940, DC's *All-Star Comics* #3, which featured eight solo stories starring DC superheroes from other anthologies, worked those eight solo stories together with a framing sequence that revealed that these eight superheroes were all part of a superhero team called the *Justice Society of America*. Thus, the concept of a shared universe was born, which in turn created shared continuity between the characters.

However, even after ostensibly introducing the idea of a shared continuity, DC kept the *shared* aspect to a minimum. For instance, while Flash and Hawkman might both be members of the Justice Society of America, they continued to each have a feature in the pages of *Flash Comics* where neither one ever acknowledged the other *nor* the Justice Society of America. Due to this approach, Batman and Superman did not interact with each other in a comic book adventure until *1952!*[4]

Things began to change in the late 1950s when editor Julius Schwartz helped launch the *Silver Age* by having the creative teams introduce new versions of the Flash and Green Lantern. These new heroes, Barry Allen and Hal Jordan would interact with each other in their respective comics, complete with footnotes referencing their earlier interactions. Soon, Flash and Green Lantern would join together with Wonder Woman, Martian Manhunter, and Aquaman

---

[3] The company was named after the first name of its three founders, Morris Coyne, Louis Silberkleit and John Goldwater.
[4] "The Mightiest Team in the World!" *Superman* Vol. 1 #76 (1952). By Edmund Hamilton and Curt Swan.

to form a new version of the Justice Society called the Justice League of America (Batman and Superman were also members, but only rarely showed up in the comics in the early years).

DC's success with superheroes led Martin Goodman and Stan Lee at Marvel Comics to decide to give superheroes another shot. The publisher had attempted several superheroes in the 1940s, most famously Captain America, Namor, and the Human Torch. Lee had attempted an aborted revival of these three heroes in the early 1950s. Now, Marvel was back doing superheroes, with Jack Kirby creating several classic heroes with Lee. Since Marvel was a good deal more streamlined than DC, with its factions of editors protecting their characters, Lee and Kirby had no problem working their heroes into a shared universe. In time, the shared universe of the Marvel Universe became one of the biggest selling points of Marvel Comics. You couldn't miss *Tales of Astonish* issue #66, as something that happened in that issue might affect *Tales of Suspense* issue #70, etc.

Once you have a shared universe, though, retcons become an important part of the shared continuity. It quickly becomes impossible for the various comic titles to coexist in a shared universe without some sort of conflict occurring. This is why the very notion of a Marvel Universe is almost inherently a lie, as there is absolutely no way to have a coherent narrative involving all of these characters being written by so many different creators. Retcons are a necessity because conflicts will come up at times and retcons exist to maintain the fiction of a coherent Marvel Universe.

The Marvel Universe is one of the most famous shared universes in popular fiction, but it is important to note that it began as a single universe. *The Fantastic Four* was Marvel's first superhero comic book of the early 1960s, and therefore, it inherently could not *share* a universe with anyone, as it *was* the universe when it debuted in late 1961.

Even when the Golden Age hero, Namor the Sub-Mariner, made his Marvel Age debut in *Fantastic Four* issue #4, it was unclear if the adventures of the Fantastic Four were supposed to share a continuity with Marvel's Golden Age comics, or if this Namor was simply, in effect, a brand new character. It was not until *Fantastic Four* issue #5, which involved a rather naked advertisement for Marvel's new ongoing series, *The Incredible Hulk*, by virtue of the Fantastic Four team member, the Human Torch, reading the Hulk's new comic in the issue, that the shared Marvel Universe was officially born.

A major retcon early in the history of the Marvel Universe was in 1964's *Avengers* #4, where Jack Kirby and Stan Lee brought back Marvel's biggest superhero star of the 1940s, Captain America. You see, while Captain America debuted before the United States entered World War II, the majority of his original series took place while the United States was at war. Once World War II ended, Captain America and Bucky returned home and continued to fight regular criminals instead of enemy armies. Eventually, Bucky was written out of the series and Captain America gained a new sidekick, Golden Girl (1948), but the writing was on the wall for the patriotic hero, and he lost his series by the end of 1949.

He was then revived in 1954, with Golden Girl retconned out and Bucky back as his sidekick. With a desire to revive the World War II-era interest in the patriotic hero Marvel had him fight Communists. It did not go over well enough, and the revival was quickly cancelled. When he returned, again, in 1964 Kirby and Lee revealed that Captain America and Bucky were trying to stop a rocket when Cap was thrown from said rocket and landed into frozen waters where he went into suspended animation for the next 20 years while Bucky was killed when the rocket exploded.

That retcon dramatically altered Captain America, as his hook now went from *patriotic superhero* to *man out of time haunted by the death of his sidekick*. Of course, later writers then examined that retcon even further by asking, "Okay, then who was the Captain America and Bucky who fought against the Communists in the 1950s?" and so created a story in which we learn who those fill-in heroes were, which led to other writers asking, "but what about the Captain America of 1945-1948? Who was that guy?" Most great retcons lead to even more retcons as different writers pick up on ideas introduced in the notable retcon.

For instance, decades later, it had become a joke that only three characters in comics would ever stay dead – Uncle Ben, Gwen Stacy, and Bucky Barnes. However, writer Ed Brubaker challenged even that maxim by having Bucky turn out to be alive and working for the Russians as an assassin named the Winter Soldier. The Winter Soldier became a popular character, and that storyline became a major part of the Marvel Cinematic Universe and comics. As expected, it led to more retcons, as we learned of the Winter Soldier's secret role in the past of the Marvel Universe. The greatest retcons inspire numerous other new stories in the shared universe.

Moench used both versions of the term as he formulated his ideal take on Marc Spector, Moon Knight.

Moench broke into comics in the early 1970s writing horror-themed stories for Warren Publishing's famous black and white horror magazines, like *Creepy* and *Eerie*. In 1974, Moench began to write for Marvel's version of those black-and-white magazines.[5] Moench was essentially the main writer of that whole line of magazines, writing horror titles such as *Haunt of Horror*, *Vampire Tales* and *Monsters Unleashed*, as well as kung fu comics like *Deadly Hands of Kung Fu* and the licensed series, *Planet of the Apes*. Moench slowly began to write for Marvel's regular colour comic books in 1974, taking over *Master of Kung Fu* from writer Steve Englehart, as well as *Werewolf by Night* from writer Mike Friedrich.

Werewolf by Night was a tricky series to write, since the lead character, Jack Russell was not really a superhero, but since he was the star of the series, he couldn't quite be a villain, either. He was simply an otherwise regular guy who was caught up in misadventures because he was a werewolf. Moench would later reflect on the complexities of writing essentially a villain as the lead of his own series, as whom do you have a villain fight? He noted, "When your 'hero' is a *monster*, your villains are often actually *heroes*. Either that or someone/something even *worse* than the monstrous character of the title. After all, who else would risk life and limb to battle werewolves, vampires, and zombies?"[6]

It was with that in mind that Moench and Don Perlin came up with a new antagonist for their werewolf character that would be directly tied into the themes of the werewolf. Since the moon turned Jack Russell into a werewolf, then Moench and Perlin would give him a moon-themed foe. Moench explained years later, "If he's going to be going up against a werewolf, he's gotta be a night character because if they're going to fight it has to be at night. Right there, night character...What else do you connect to a werewolf? The moon. That spelt out the colours of the costume. Jet and silver. Black and white."[7] In

---

[5] Dubbed the Curtis Magazines, after Marvel's distributor at the time, Curtis Circulation Company, which was an affiliated company of Marvel.

[6] "Shades of the Moon." *Moon Knight* Vol. 1 #15 (1981). By Doug Moench, Bill Sienkiewicz, and Christie Scheele.

[7] "The Conversation: Charlie Huston and Doug Moench." Comic Foundry, 2006. comicfoundry.blogspot.com/2006/04/

Werewolf by Night issue #32, The Committee, a corrupt group of Los Angeles businessmen who wanted to take control of a werewolf, hire mercenary Marc Spector (originally spelt Mark Spector by mistake) to capture Jack Russell for them. The group then supplied Spector with the Moon Knight costume, as well as the name *Moon Knight*. Amusingly, Spector initially mocked how dumb the name sounded, but he could use the $10,000 bounty, so he accepted their deal. Moon Knight hunted Russell in a helicopter flown by an associate, Frenchie.

After successfully capturing Russell at the end of *Werewolf by Night* issue #32, Spector revealed that he wasn't such a bad guy in the following issue when he had second thoughts about essentially selling a human being to a group of villains. So, Moon Knight freed Russell and the two then tore The Committee apart and parted as, if not friends, certainly not enemies. At the time, Moon Knight was nominally just a one-off character, but Moench recalled, "[E]ven then I suspected we'd stumbled onto something a wee bit more significant than just another WWBN villain."[8] That belief was shared with Marvel's then-Editor-in-Chief, Marv Wolfman, who suggested to Moench that he and Perlin adapt Moon Knight into a superhero.

The process of turning a quasi-villain into a superhero led to the first of Moench's retcons. You see, supervillains typically do not require much in the way of a background. If you look at Spider-Man's earliest rogues, their backgrounds were almost all, "Gain superpowers, get a costume and begin committing crimes." Similarly, when Moon Knight was a Werewolf by Night villain, all you needed to know was that he had a moon-themed costume and some weapons specifically geared towards fighting werewolves (like a spiked battle glove called a cestus that was coated in silver). A superhero, however, needs a lot more than that and the character is often given that *something more* through retcons.

This is most notably clear in the case of two high-profile superheroes who debuted as antagonists of other characters: Wolverine and Deadpool. Wolverine debuted in 1974's *Incredible Hulk* #180-81 as a new foe for the Hulk. Created by Len Wein, John Romita, and Roy Thomas, we learned very little about Wolverine in that first story besides the fact that he was Canadian, he was scrappy, and he had cool looking claws. Wein then brought the Canadian

---

[8] "Shades of the Moon." *Moon Knight* Vol. 1 #15 (1981). By Doug Moench, Bill Sienkiewicz and Christie Scheele.

hero into an all-new, all-different international team of X-Men in 1975's *Giant-Size X-Men* #1. Wein, though, left the ongoing X-Men series that spun out of *Giant-Size X-Men* after plotting just a single story arc. It would be incoming writer, Chris Claremont, working with artist Dave Cockrum (who had co-created most of the new X-Men characters with Wein), who would use retcons to create several interesting early contradictions from Wein's original conception of Wolverine.

Wein pictured Wolverine as a young man who had gloves with claws on. Claremont and Cockrum instead revealed in *X-Men* issue #98 that Wolverine was an adult whose claws were part of his body. Claremont and Cockrum also planned to reveal that Wolverine was not a typical mutant, but rather an actual wolverine who had been mutated into a humanoid via the previously introduced geneticist anti-hero, the High Evolutionary. That idea was dropped, but it was later used as the original origin for a new superhero in 1976 called Spider-Woman... until that, too, was retconned and Jessica Drew was no longer a mutated spider who became Spider-Woman but rather a woman with spider powers.

Over the years, Claremont used retcons to add more and more details to Wolverine's background, especially as Canadian artist John Byrne replaced Cockrum on the series and made Wolverine a bit of a passion project. Byrne and Claremont retconned Wolverine's original powers of being scrappy and hard to hurt and expanded them to mean that he had healing powers. Those healing powers, in turn, were retconned over time to be more and more significant, until writer Marc Guggenheim had Wolverine survive an explosion that briefly left him as just a skeleton in a *Civil War* tie-in in 2006.

When Wolverine was introduced, there were no indications he was anything but the age that he appeared to be. However, Claremont dropped hints that Wolverine was a lot older than he looked until 1990's *Uncanny X-Men* #268 officially revealed that Wolverine knew Captain America during World War II, and Wolverine still looks the same now as he did back then. In a 1986 *Alpha Flight* story, writer Bill Mantlo revealed, through a retcon, that Wolverine did not know how his claws came to be coated in the unbreakable metal known as Adamantium. That was the first hint that Wolverine *might* not have all of his memories. Up until that point, Wolverine never seemed to have any problems remembering his past. In 1991's *Wolverine* #48-50, Larry Hama went a step further and retconned *all* of Wolverine's established history by revealing that most of his memories were fake. They had been implanted by Department K, the secretive agency that turned him into Weapon X and gave him the Adamantium skeleton, an event that was first revealed earlier that year in a *Marvel Comics Presents* story by Barry Windsor-Smith.[9]

The more popular Wolverine has become, the more retcons that have followed him around, including the famous cliché now that Wolverine has somehow run into nearly every major Marvel character at one point in their past before they became famous heroes. Heck, he even had a team-up with Richard and Mary Parker, the spies who were Peter Parker's parents (before leaving young Peter with Richard's brother, Ben, and his wife, May, before Richard and Mary were killed).

That has mostly been the experience of Deadpool, as well. Introduced by Rob Liefeld as basically an "Evil Spider-Man" in 1990's *New Mutants* issue #98. The wise-cracking assassin tangled with the young mutant heroes known as The New Mutants, along with their new mentor, Cable, and his old flame, Domino.

Like Wein and Wolverine, Liefeld had a background in mind for Deadpool, but just as Wein left *X-Men* before he could implement any of it, so, too, did Liefeld leave *X-Force* (which was a re-titled *New Mutants*, spotlighting the evolution of the young mutants into more of a paramilitary strike force) before anything but the bare bone details of Deadpool could be introduced.[10] Like Claremont and Wolverine, it was Nicieza who gave Deadpool a real name. Amusingly, Nicieza felt that Deadpool reminded him of the New Teen Titans arch-rival, Deathstroke the Terminator, whose real name was Slade Wilson, so Nicieza gave Deadpool the real name of Wade Wilson. Liefeld always insisted that Deathstroke did not play a factor in the creation of Deadpool, citing instead Spider-Man, Snake-Eyes, and Boba Fett, but Nicieza naming Deadpool Wade Wilson has made it so that the comparison between Deadpool and Deathstroke will never go away.

While Nicieza was the main Deadpool writer for several years, it wasn't until Deadpool received his own ongoing series in 1997, written by Joe Kelly, that his background was developed in full. Kelly used several issues to reveal how Wade Wilson was dying of cancer while he was experimented on by

---

[9] "Weapon X." *Marvel Comics Presents* Vol. 1 #72-84 (1991). By Barry Windsor-Smith.

[10] Rob Liefeld revealed that Deadpool had a connection to Department K and its Weapon X program but gave no details.

Department K to possibly be part of a new Weapon X program. When he failed that program, he was sent with a group of other rejects to be further experimented on. As the various subjects died, there would be a "dead pool" as to which subject would die first. Since Wade was already dying, almost everyone bet on him. Instead, during one round of seemingly fatal torture, it kickstarted his healing powers, making it so that he could not die and thus would always be the winner of the "dead pool." Tragically, the same process that made it so that he would never die also made it so that his skin would be constantly covered with cancerous tumours.

The big difference, then, between Moon Knight and these other adversaries-turned-superheroes, is that it was Moon Knight's creator who was doing these retcons. In *Marvel Spotlight* issue #28, Moench gave Marc Spector a whole new background and an additional two aliases! Perhaps inspired by the classic pulp hero of the 1930s, The Shadow, who also employed multiple aliases, Moench revealed that Marc Spector had invested the money that he had made as a mercenary and had become a millionaire, using the alias Steven Grant to do his business dealings and society gatherings. As Steven Grant, he had a personal assistant, Marlene Fontaine, whom he was also dating. Spector also adopted the alias of Jake Lockley, a salt of the Earth taxi driver, whom Spector used to pick up information from the street. In his Lockley identity, he befriended Crawley, a homeless man who fed him information from the street, and Gena, a woman who ran a diner that Lockley frequented, so that people could contact him and leave him information through Gena.

Since he was no longer *just* a werewolf opponent, Moench and Perlin dropped the spiked silver gloves that would be a bit too violent for regular criminals and also revealed that Russell had bitten Moon Knight during their fight. As a result, Moon Knight had super-strength based on the phases of the moon (when it was full, he had significant super-strength, but when it was just a quarter moon, he would have a quarter of that strength, and so on), also designing a glider cape for Moon Knight, allowing him to effectively fly.

When Moon Knight received his regular backup feature in *Hulk! Magazine*, Perlin had other assignments, so after Gene Colan and Keith Pollard drew the first two instalments, Bill Sienkiewicz took over the feature with *Hulk! Magazine* issue #13. Editor Ralph Macchio did not like the glider cape, so Sienkiewicz designed a new cape. Due to his new cape and Sienkiewicz's heavily Neal Adams-inspired artwork, Moon Knight, for the first time, began to evoke Batman in his design.

Few things are quite as important to a good superhero as a well-defined origin. You might notice that when superheroes are adapted into superhero films, they almost always adapt the origin story. This is because origin stories are both important in explaining who a superhero is, but also, they tend to be highly compelling stories in their own right.

Superman's origin was essentially told in just a single page in *Action Comics* #1, revealing that he was the only survivor of the destroyed planet Krypton, giving Superman a classical origin that fit both Greek, Roman, and Biblical mythology. A year later, Superman issue #1 expanded that origin to further explore the role of Ma and Pa Kent in adopting the young alien infant. Later stories were retconned to include more detail. Superman did not know he was an alien until more than a decade into his comic book career, and we didn't even learn the story of Krypton's destruction until Superman's 10th anniversary in 1948.

Unlike Superman and many other notable superheroes (including Captain America, Spider-Man, the Fantastic Four, and Wonder Woman), Batman was not introduced with an origin. However, it took just six months before Bill Finger and Bob Kane revealed that young Bruce Wayne saw his parents murdered in front of his eyes as a child. He vowed right then and there to avenge his parents' murder and studied and trained himself to become a crime fighter. One night, a bat flew into his den, and he realized that criminals are *a cowardly and superstitious lot*, so he decided to dress up as a bat to scare them.

During the Golden Age, superhero origins were often things that happened to superheroes. For instance, Superman was born with superpowers. Captain America was given a Super-Soldier Serum that gave him his powers. Billy Batson wandered into a magical subway where he was given the powers of Shazam to become Captain Marvel. Batman stood out among those characters for his origin involving him actively deciding to make himself into a superhero. However, in the Silver Age, Marvel made a name for itself with origins that were often based on personal guilt. For instance, while Peter Parker might have gained superpowers by accidentally being bitten by a spider, he didn't become a superhero until his beloved Uncle Ben was murdered by a criminal that Peter could have stopped had he not decided that it wasn't his responsibility to stop a criminal. Once Ben died and Peter realized who the killer was, Spider-Man's whole mantra centred around "With great power comes great responsibility."

Other Marvel heroes had similar origins in which their mistakes eventually led to them becoming heroes. Reed Richards stole a rocket ship and accidentally exposed himself and his closest friends to cosmic rays which led to them becoming the Fantastic Four. Tony Stark sold munitions for war until he himself was almost killed in a war zone, leading him to create a suit of armour to survive and then fight crime as Iron Man. Doctor Stephen Strange was a cocky surgeon whose reckless behaviour left him with injured hands. In a quest to heal himself, he instead became the Master of Mystic Arts. These origins were powerful parts of each respective hero's story and, as shown with Wolverine and Deadpool, when the initial origin is either bland or nebulous, retcons were used to improve the origins. Like Frank Miller revealing that Matt Murdock didn't just gain superpowers in the accident that blinded him as a kid, but was also trained as a sort of ninja by a mysterious mentor named Stick, or Jack Kirby and Stan Lee revealing that Dr Don Blake didn't just happen to find a walking stick that was secretly a hammer that turned him into Thor, but rather, Don Blake *was* Thor, punished by his father, Odin, to live his life as a human until he learned humility and once he had done, he was rewarded by becoming Thor again.

Similarly, now that Moon Knight was graduating from his popular *Hulk! Magazine* back-ups into his own ongoing series, Moench realised the need to give Moon Knight a better origin than *some bad guys paid him to become Moon Knight and gave him the suit*. So, in Moon Knight issue #1, Moench gave Marc Spector his own classic *mistakes leading to a hero* Marvel origin through some major retcons. Now, while working as a soldier of fortune, Spector ran with a group led by the vicious Raul Bushman. When doing a job at the Egyptian border, the mercenaries came across an archaeologist named Dr Peter Alraune. Alraune objected to Bushman ordering the looting of the local temples and tried to kill Bushman, but Marc stopped him, and Bushman then murdered him. Alraune's daughter, Marlene, tried to avenge her father's death, but Marc stopped her and saved her life while claiming personal responsibility for the death of her father. Bushman then ordered his men to murder some locals and Marc objected. Bushman owed him for saving his life from Alraune's attack, so he *spared* Marc by just having him beaten and left to die in the middle of the desert. Marc dragged himself to a temple where Marlene was hiding out with a local tribe and Marc then apparently died, in front of a statue honouring the Egyptian god, Khonshu. Marc, seemingly resurrected, took on the identity of Moon Knight. He defeated Bushman and avenged the death of Marlene's father. This was how Marlene came to know Marc.

Page 6 of *Moon Knight* Vol. 1 #4 (1980).

This was a much more memorable origin and, sure enough, much like other superheroes, such as Spider-Man and Doctor Strange, Moon Knight's origin gets revisited frequently in the comics and media adaptations of the character.

You might note that this new origin directly contradicts his first appearance. So, in *Moon Knight* issue #4, Moench came up with a convoluted explanation for how Marc was hired by the Committee. As it turned out, the Committee had reformed and had hired a series of assassins to kill Marc as revenge for his betrayal back in *Werewolf by Night* issue #33. When Marlene inquired as to why the Committee was out to get them, Marc explained that he had decided to investigate The Committee a few years earlier. Marc had Frenchie infiltrate the group and Frenchie convinced The Committee that he had come up with both the name Moon Knight and the design of the costume and then they *hired* Marc Spector to become Moon Knight, despite him already being Moon Knight.

Earlier, Frank Miller's Daredevil run was referenced regarding how Miller altered Daredevil's origin, but Miller's run was also important for how Miller used retcons to re-centre Daredevil as a more tragic hero. In his first issue as writer/artist on *Daredevil* issue #168 in 1980, Miller used a retcon to reveal that Matt Murdock had a long-lost love named Elektra who was then introduced into the series as an assassin torn between her mission and her love for Matt. Miller used this retcon, as well as the aforementioned retcon that showed that Matt was tied to a never-before-mentioned mentor, Stick, who was part of a mystical group known as the Chaste, who were at war with a villainous group known as the Hand, to guide Daredevil away from standard superhero-style stories and re-centre him on this new mixture of martial arts and noir storytelling.

The aforementioned retcons involving Captain America and Thor, which revealed that Captain America never made it out of World War II and that Dr Don Blake did not turn into Thor, but rather was always Thor himself, also re-centred those respective heroes, with Captain America now being a *Man out of a Time* and Thor going away from superhero adventures to explore the god side of his character (as Jack Kirby was always more interested in Norse mythology than Thor as a superhero, anyways).

Similarly, Moench's concept of the *Moon Knight* series was that Moon Knight was a *regular* adventurer, in the sense that his villains and his stories tended away from superpowered foes and things of that nature. It was closer to James Bond style than, say, Spider-Man (this was very similar to Moench's approach to Shang-Chi's adventures in his long *Master of Kung Fu* run with artists Paul Gulacy, Mike Zeck, and Gene Day). Therefore, in *Moon Knight* #6, we are shown Moon Knight having some trouble defeating a group of criminals. He then revealed to Marlene that the werewolf virus that had given him super-strength had finally fully faded away and he was back to being a normal human again. Moench had successfully used a retcon to re-centre Moon Knight as a normal hero and moved him away from the werewolf-powered supernatural fighter he was when he was first introduced.

As seen throughout these many different superhero examples, retcons have been a major tool for superhero comic book writers in both redefining former antagonists as heroes, as well as honing the *hook* on certain characters via high-concept origins. However, the reason that Moench's Moon Knight stands out is that it was Moench who was doing all of this.

Outside of, perhaps, Bill Finger and Bob Kane giving Batman an origin six months after he debuted, or Jerry Siegel and Joe Shuster expanding Superman's origin from half a page in 1938's *Action Comics* #1 to two pages in 1939's *Superman* issue #1, the same creators who introduce a character are not the ones who are doing dramatic retcons altering the character.

As shown with Wolverine and Deadpool, it wasn't until their respective creators had stopped having control over them that both characters were dramatically revamped; with Deadpool's biggest evolution as a character not happening until three other writers had been in control of the character.

Moon Knight, though, had his creator dramatically shift the character from a werewolf fighter to a James Bond-esque adventurer and redo his origin, making it an origin truly fit for a Marvel Comics superhero. With all of the retcons to his own work, Moench did more to re-conceptualize his own superhero than any other Marvel comic book writer before him or since.

From the Dead and Drawing a Line in the Sand

by Scott Weatherly

Marvel NOW! was a Marvel initiative started in 2012, to provide a jumping-on point for new readers. It was a chance to revamp existing characters and introduce new ones. These initiatives are ten a penny in the big two, we readers have gotten so used to them that they just flow over us, for the most part. However, in the glut of revamps that will be forgotten and dropped, a couple of new series stick and reframe a character going forward. The Moon Knight series started as part of Marvel NOW! in 2014 is one such series.

The team of Warren Ellis, Declan Shalvey, and Jordie Bellaire understood the assignment and gave us a six-issue run that established a new baseline for the character, which is still being felt almost 10 years later.

The art and colouring of the run are exceptional and worthy of all the praise they received. However, I intend to examine and assess how Warren Ellis used this run to link to the past, reframe it and build the new baseline for Moon Knight.

More than almost any other character in the Marvel universe, Moon Knight has gone through changes with each new series. This ability to change is a double edge sword. It makes Moon Knight an exciting and adaptable character, but it also means that following his canonical history is a tough task. His comic career in the 2000s and early 2010s is sporadic and disjointed. There had been three series before Ellis, starting with 2006s *Moon Knight* (Charlie Huston & David Finch), followed by *Vengeance of the Moon Knight* in 2009 (Greg Hurwitz & Jerome Opeña), and then *Moon Knight* (again) in 2011 (Brian Michael Bendis & Alex Maleev). Apart from the first two story arcs of the 2006 Moon Knight, none of these made much of a splash. In fact, the 2011 series by Bendis and Maleev is often derided by Moon Knight fans.

Reading these series, it's clear that Marvel wasn't sure what to do with Moon Knight and was searching for a hook and set-up to build upon. With Marvel NOW! Warren Ellis was given an opportunity to clear the decks and create a new era for Moon Knight. He takes this opportunity and runs with it. What we get is the six-issue run that is collected as *From the Dead*.

From the Dead is an interesting choice and can be interpreted in multiple ways. Of course, the first thought is that Marc Spector was brought back from the dead, by Khonshu. This has been disputed over the years, but, in the first issue of this series, Ellis introduces a new psychiatrist who explains to Marc "I believe you were raised from the dead by an outerterrestrial entity and remade to some extent by that … you're not crazy. Your brain has been colonized by an ancient consciousness from beyond space-time."[1] Ellis is establishing a new status quo for the relationship between Marc and Khonshu, as well as Marc's mental illness and ostensibly confirming that Marc was raised from the dead.

A more inside-baseball and arrogant interpretation is that Ellis believed this collection is pulling Moon Knight out of the downward cycle he was trapped in. These six issues are saving Moon Knight from irrelevance and becoming a forgotten character, comic book death. This is a chance to save him from being the dead.

Finally (and getting to the hypothesis of this essay), this title defines Ellis's approach to each of the six issues and how they explore how past things, thought forgotten and dead, can come back to haunt us. How they need to be purged before we can embark on a new era of our lives. Each of the issues in this short run do just that. Within the stories, we are presented with past events impacting and coming to a resolution, while also making clear and distinct links to Moon Knight's first self-titled run, written by Doug Moench. This

---

[1] "Slasher." *Moon Knight* Vol. 7 #1 (2014). By Warren Ellis, Declan Shalvey, Jordie Belaire.

run is a line in the sand, acknowledging the past, but also stating that this is a new century and Moon Knight is ready to slip into a new suit to meet it.

The first issue of the run, titled "Slasher", opens with exposition panels highlighting Moon Knight's previous run and his canonical origin. Giving the reader a baseline for what has gone before and where this series will jump from. This transitions, to a crime scene and a character that was first introduced By Doug Moench in issue #12 of volume 1, Detective Flint. This is the first indication that Ellis is pulling from the past. This original run character is then joined by the *all-new* Moon Knight, or as he is to be addressed in his new three-piece suit, Mr Knight.

Mr Knight struts into the book with confidence. A blaze of white in a grimy New York Alley. Flint addresses him as *Mr Knight*, highlighting that this relationship has been going on for some time. He then proceeds to explain that the investigation is about a slasher killer, just like one of their first cases. It should be noted, however, that the introduction of Flint was for a monster villain, Morpheus, not a slasher killer. The comparison to be drawn for this issue comes a little earlier, issue #2 of volume 1, "The Slasher."

The slasher of the original run is killing homeless men, each time declaring that the victim is not *the one*. It is revealed that *the one* the killer is looking for is the father that abandoned him as a child. The issue covers a period of weeks if not months as the killings continue and Moon Knight struggles to deduce who the killer is and stop him. He eventually concedes, and reveals his identity to his network of allies, asking them to help catch the killer. It's a big moment for Moon Knight, bringing these people in and asking for help. It's portrayed as a defining moment for how Moon Knight will operate, as part of a team that will help him repeatedly.

In contrast, Ellis quickly demonstrates that this ethic has been shed. In fact, the isolation of Marc and Moon Knight will continue as a theme throughout the series, culminating in a final statement in issue six.

To establish his isolation Moon Knight is introduced in the back of a large driverless limo. This vehicle is designed, usually, for large groups, in this case, it is populated by a lone individual. This is further highlighted when a police officer addresses Mr Knight and states that he cannot go after the killer, as he is not a police officer. Mr Knight explains "Officer, I appreciate your perspective. But I'm talking about going underground into the hide of a highly trained killer, which will be where he keeps all his weapons. I'd prefer to do that part for

Moon Knight strolls confidently on page 5 of *Moon Knight* Vol. 7 #1 (2014).

you."[2] Mr Knight understands the dangers and wants to keep people safe. He is isolating himself, knowing what has happened to people in the past.

Moreover, I mentioned before that Moon Knight had to bring in his team as a way of cracking the case. This requirement is also shed by Ellis. Mr Knight is shown to be a skilled detective, reading the scene, and building up a profile of the crime and criminal. He no longer has a need for a network of agents, he can read the evidence in front of him. He is self-sufficient and we will see, even more lethal.

To bring home the sense of connection, in the original run Moench has it revealed that the killer is Crawley's son. Crawley is *the one* the killer has been looking for. To explain he recounts how he became an alcoholic, and his actions drove his wife and son away. This brings the theme of connection and family to a head, making the slasher killer a family affair, for both Crawley and now the wider group. The story culminates with the killer caught and being brought to justice, teasing a possible redemption and reconnection between Crawley and his son. However, this is not to be, as the killer breaks free and accidentally falls from a roof to his death, despite Moon Knight's best efforts to save him. The final panel has Crawley take responsibility for what he did and didn't do for his son while being surrounded by his new family.

Ellis's killer is also a result of family abandonment but of a different kind. It is revealed that the killer is a former agent of S.H.I.E.L.D. that was injured in the line of duty and discharged. He has been left with debilitating injuries and his S.H.I.E.L.D. family refuses to *fix* him. He is now killing people for their body parts to rebuild himself. Taking people that he saw as wasting their gym-trained bodies. He is tied to a sense of duty and service to his country.

Ellis is touching on the same idea as Moench, the notion of the family you build rather than the one you are born to. However, where Moench presents a family coming together, Ellis presents a victim of what happens when a family member is no longer useful. For a comic released in 2014, after over 10 years fighting in the Middle East, and endless stories of soldiers being injured and sent home, suffering mental and physical pain, it's not hard to see the parallel Ellis is making to the American military. This connection is strengthened by Bellaire's colours, as the scene is coloured only in red, white and blue. In addition to this, Moon Knight was looking to save Crawley's son, hoping for

---

[2] Ibid.

justice rather than death. In 2014 Mr Knight takes out the killer with lethal efficiency.

As an epilogue to the story, we get the scene with the doctor and a return to Grant mansion. This short set of panels tops off the statement Ellis has been making. The mansion is cold, littered with cobwebs, and empty but for Marc, his alters, and Khonshu watching on. The final spoken words of the issue are from Khonshu, "you are my son."[3] This is no longer the colourful family base of Team Moon Knight.

With Moon Knight being re-established in issue #1 Ellis throws the reader straight into a new story with the killing, page by page, of eight people in issue #2. A wonderful artistic choice, on each page a panel becomes white space following a killing. However, each panel tells a small part of the victim's story and how they are employees of the same company and have little in the way of functional family life. In addition, each white space becomes populated with a snippet of information from another's story, that of the sniper, killing the people we are following.

From this information, we learn that the killer is taking revenge for being abandoned and left for dead, after years of Service. Echoing the slasher from the first issue. However, where the slasher was a result of injury, this abandonment is due to a departmental shutdown. He was an asset that was no longer needed like a piece of machinery being left in an abandoned office.

Ellis is drawing from issue #17 of the Moench run, "Master Sniper's Legacy," and again we are presented with killers that parallel and contrast each other. Moench's Master Sniper is the fanatical acolyte of the leader of a rogue nation-state. He crosses paths with Moon Knight after killing an old friend of Marc Spector. The story becomes about two personal causes. Chasing down the killer of a friend and commitment to a leader and ideology. Once again Moench is creating a story that weaves in a personal connection and emotion. In contrast, there is no personal connection for Ellis's Moon Knight. He witnesses the shootings and confronts the sniper. It's chance that Moon Knight was there to witness the shootings, but he is still committed to bringing down the shooter. Moench gives Moon Knight a personal motivation to keep fighting. While Ellis gives the reader a Moon Knight that will go to extremes of violence

---

[3] Ibid.

and combat because that is just what he does. He doesn't need the emotional kickstart.

Coming back to the two snipers. As highlighted Master Sniper was a devotee of an ideology, however, he is still just a weapon for said cause. He is given direction and let off the leash to do the bidding of a superior, who dictates the direction of the ideology. It is also indicated that he is just one of several killers used by the rogue nation-state. As with Ellis' sniper, he is the tool of a government, being used to do their dirty work. The difference is Master Sniper believes, in some twisted way, what is doing is just. He even states "I serve Nimrod Strange, the greatest man who ever lived! And even if you stop me, Moon knight, the Third World Slayers will go on…until the world's brought to its knees!"[4]

In comparison, Ellis's sniper knows he was a tool, and it was a job, but he was good at it "It may not have been a good life, but it was my life. They took it…"[5] He has no delusions of ideology; he was just being paid for his skills. I would even suggest Ellis's Sniper is a cautionary tale for Master Sniper. While he is useful and devoted, he will be taken care of, however, he could just as easily be cast aside when there is no further use for him.

As to the fate of our two snipers', these further demonstrate Ellis's approach, that the past is something that cannot be hidden and must be confronted to move on. Master Sniper is killed fighting Moon Knight when his gun fires and the shot starts an avalanche. Moench makes it clear that Moon Knight is not to blame for this death. Much like the accidental death of the Slasher in issue #2, Moench manipulates events to keep Moon Knight's hands clean. It should be noted though that Moon Knight does go after those that sent Master Sniper, bringing Nimrod Strange down in issue #20. That death is also not caused by Moon Knight. As Nimrod kills himself by taking out a tanker full of explosives. Justice is served, vengeance is satisfied, and Moon Knight is still a *hero*.

Ellis's sniper is also killed, and while it is not at the hands of Moon Knight, it has different implications. Following the sniper's confession, both he and Moon

---

[4] "Master Sniper's Legacy." *Moon Knight* Vol. 1 #17 (1982). By Doug Moench, Bill Sienkiewicz, Christie Scheele.

[5] "Sniper." *Moon Knight* Vol. 7 #2 (2014). By Warren Ellis, Declan Shalvey, Jordie Belaire.

Knight are confronted by a final member of the team that operated the sniper. He pulls out a gun and shoots the injured sniper in the head. He then gives Moon Knight a short explanation. They left security services to join financial services, simply to make money. They always saw the sniper as a tool, he wasn't supposed to shoot them. He finishes by saying "The bank always wins."[6] There was no ideology, no grand idea, just services, and the fact more money could be made elsewhere.

Master Sniper is a product of the 80s. A world divided by two superpowers and their conflicting ideologies. A world that had already been scared by ideology, and devotion to a cause. Ellis's Sniper is a product of the early 21st century and war for profit. The final statement regarding banks winning, being made in 2014 following the 2008 global financial crisis, can be interpreted as another dig by Ellis. There is no wider rogue group of ideologues to chase down and bring to comic book justice. Those directing the snipers and altering world events now sit in boardrooms, banks, and government offices. Moon Knight is left with no one to fight; the bank has already won. He is not just isolated from family; he is isolated from a larger mission.

Of all six of the issues in the run, issue #3, 'Box', has the clearest ties to the Moench run, and the message of confronting the past. In the first dialogue exchange of the issue, a character states "That music. Reminds me of something from when I was a kid."[7] Straight away indicating that we are dealing with something from the past. The next third of the story is a confrontation between people, Moon Knight and four punk ghosts. They are depicted as you would expect stereotypical punk gang members to look, they could have stepped off the set of *The Warriors*, and they have come out to play.

Moon Knight confronts them as Mr Knight and finds that he is unable to hit them, while they can hit, kick and whip him. Forced to retreat, Marc is advised by Khonshu that he is the avatar of "A civilization of the dead as much as the living"[8] and that he has in his possession garments that will allow him to fight the dead. While digging through boxes of artefacts Marc mentions that "I don't remember buying most of this." to which Khonshu replies "Perhaps you weren't

---

[6] Ibid.

[7] "Box." *Moon Knight* Vol. 7 #3 (2014). By Warren Ellis, Declan Shalvey, and Jordie Belaire.

[8] Ibid.

supposed to remember."[9] This raises a question about Moon Knight's relationship with his past. This could be taken as a meta-commentary on the changing continuity, and how writers pick and choose what stays and what goes. However, if we tie it to Ellis's commentary that we do choose or are manipulated to forget certain things. However, they are still there to be found and reintroduced or resolved.

In this case, they are reintroduced, as Marc adorns himself in a suit of Artifacts and bones, literally connecting him to the dead. Gaining powers from the dead he successfully confronts the punk ghosts. When Marc stepped out of his limo as Mr Knight, he is a representation of the modern, with gadgets and rationale, ready to deal with material threats (snipers and slasher killers). He acknowledges his past and his disconnection from it when he states that he does not remember attaining the items. It is only when he reconnects with that past, not only his own but that of Khonshu and his culture that is he able to confront the immaterial.

Not only does Moon Knight successfully confront the ghosts he tracks them to an abandoned building, set for renovation. There he finds five sets of skeletal remains, all wearing punk attire. Four with bullet wounds to their skulls, and one holding a gun, also with a bullet wound, clearly self-inflicted. At his feet is a cracked music box, in which the ghosts are hiding. On it is written "Johnny be good, from Mom."

The layers of the past in this are threefold. First is the abandoned building in which they are found. Reflective of how old areas of cities are forgotten and allowed to fall to decay until they can be gentrified. The identity of the past is painted over so something clean and new can be presented. The second is the skeletal remains. These have been in this building, unfound for years. A violent event from the past has leaked into the present to be dealt with. Even if the bodies had been found by the renovation team, the scene would have had to have been investigated and resolved before the gentrification could progress.

Finally, the message on the music box goes back to an even earlier time, an innocent childhood lost to violence. Even as we live, we must reconcile with who we were when we were younger and how those that love us see us as we grow up and make choices. In this case, a choice was made, and a violent end was taken as the only solution to reconcile with the Johnny that had been good.

---

[9] Ibid.

Moreover, this could be seen as a reminder to Moon Knight. Don't forget the times you were on a path to redemption and doing good. The fact that Moon Knight throws the box into the river indicates that he is not only discarding the ghostly past but also rejecting this reminder to be good. This is a new era, and we have a *modern* Moon Knight.

This issue is deeply linked with issues #31 and #32 of Moench's run. I would go so far as to suggest that this story was directly inspired by the cover is issue #31, which depicts Moon Knight fighting with a ghost emanating from a music box.

Issues #31 (A box of Music for Savage Studs) and #32 (When the music stops...) cover a two-part story about a young man called Lenny who struggles with his position in a New York street gang, versus his position within the local community. His gang, the Savage Studs, are running a protection racket. However, the local business owners start standing up for themselves. As tension grows into confrontation Moon Knight steps in, attempting to be a voice of reason, but is unable to prevent an accidental death.

Lenny's struggle with his conscience is the anchor of the story. Following a fight, Moon Knight confronts Lenny about what he is doing to the community he grew up in. Lenny, and in turn, Moench, lays out the state of things for young people fighting to get out of poverty in the early 80s. Surrounded by urban decay and few opportunities they are trying to take control of their lives in the only way they see possible.

To raise money and prevent further confrontation with the local businesses Lenny decides to pawn a music box, bought for his mother when he was a child. Unfortunately, this is not enough and when the leader of the Savage Studs threatens the pawnshop owner, Lenny tries to prevent the attack, but the shop keep is still killed in the tussle. Lenny is left to deal with the consequence of the decisions he has made.

The Music box found by Moon Knight in the Ellis run could just have easily stated 'Lenny be good'. Once again Ellis is linking back to issues of the original run and jumping off for his own story. Moench used the two-issue story to comment on the social impact of urban neglect and presented Moon Knight with a chance to further his redemption by helping someone make better choices, even if the larger problem can't be addressed. Ellis however is poking a hole in the gloss of the modern, to reveal the decayed history that still exists underneath.

It's not unintentional that the issue opens with a same sex couple, arm in arm, being the first to encounter the ghosts. Something that has become the norm but is in real historic terms has only been an accepted feature of society in the 21st century. This is paralleled with the building to be renovated. A remnant of the old ready to be brought into the modern. However, it hides that dark violet story that is the source of the ghosts. The ghosts of young people that may have been driven to make poor choices by living with the urban decay that is being covered up and forgotten.

It is perfectly fine and should in fact be encouraged for a city to grow and progress, as should Moon Knight. However, you must remember what has come before and not allow history to be purposely papered over. As Khonshu suggests, sometimes people make it, so we're not supposed to remember our past, individually and as a community.

While issue #3 could almost be a sequel to the Moench run, issue #4 makes more tangential, yet continuity-based, connections, while still fitting with Ellis's theme of confronting the past. The reader is introduced to Dr Skelton, who is conducting sleep and dream research, however, all his patients are experiencing the same troubling dreams. Skelton has been directed to contact Mr Knight because of his work, as Moon Knight, with Dr Peter Alraune and his patient Robert Markham, creations of Moench in the original run.

Dr Alraune (the brother of Marlene Alraune) conducted work that mutated Markham and his sleep illness, turning him into the monstrous villain, Morpheus. Morpheus appeared in issues #12 (the first appearance of Detective Flint), #22 and #23, before being defeated. In issue #23, Morpheus's defeat is a result of Dr Alraune's sacrifice. He acknowledges his work created the monster, and he has a responsibility for it. Therefore, while issue #3 was an implied follow-up, #4 is a direct continuation of those past issues.

After the initial discussion, Skelton takes Moon Knight to his lab and in a quiet room Mr Knight falls asleep to enter the realm of dreams. In that realm, Moon Knight discovers the spectral form of a former patient. The world around the patient has taken on a fungal appearance, and the patient is unable to escape. As he passes through the fungal dream realm Moon Knight hears "Cryptococcus and dimethyltryptamine," giving our detective, Mr Knight, enough explanation for what has happened.[10]

Cryptococcus is a spore fungus that can infect humans and become Cryptococcosis, or Cryptococcus Meningitis. These will affect the lungs and other tissue areas, potentially even the brain.[11]

Dimethyltryptamine, or DMT, is a molecule that can be found in certain plants. It is often used to make hallucinogenic drinks, such as ayahuasca. Ayahuasca translates from Quechua as *"vine of the spirits"* highlighting its use to perceive a different plain of experience. During the mid-20th century, it was found that small amounts of DMT are produced by the human body.[12] Also, experiments were conducted using controlled doses of DMT on patients, to record its effects on human biology and perception.

One such researcher was Dr Rick Strassman who conducted experiments in the 1990s and proposed a connection between DMT psychoactive experiences, dreaming and near-death experiences.[13] This proposition has been extended by some to suggest that taking DMT can allow us to see and experience other levels of reality.

What Moon Knight has uncovered is a patient that has died from a form of Cryptococcosis while under the influence of DMT, and the heightened DMT amount has accentuated his dream state to that of a spectral afterlife. Ripping up the floorboards he finds the body of the said patient, deducing that Skelton hid the body.

Skelton and Dr Alraune are both presented with the monster created by their work. However, where Alraune was willing to sacrifice himself to redeem his mistakes, Skelton attempted to hide them. Skelton is literally confronted with the skeleton in the closet. The thing from the past that is hidden away, so he could continue with his future. Moreover, it can be suggested that Moon

---

[10] "Sleep." *Moon Knight* Vol. 7 #4 (2014). By Warren Ellis, Declan Shalvey, and Jordie Belaire.

[11] Bennett, John E. Cryptococcosis (Cryptococcus neoformans and Cryptococcus gattii). Science Direct, 2020.
www.sciencedirect.com/topics/immunology-and-microbiology/cryptococcus

[12] Duke, L. "Discarnate entities and dimethyltryptamine (DMT): Psychopharmacology, phenomenology, and ontology." *The Journal of the American Society for Psychical Research*, 2011. Pages 26-42.

[13] Strassman, Risk. *DMT: The Spirit Molecule: A Doctor's Revolutionary Research into the Biology of Near-Death and Mystical Experiences*. Park Street Press, 2007.

Knight's reconnection with his supernatural side in the previous issue allows him to solve this case.

Issue #5 of the Ellis run is possibly the most violent issue of the run, with influences from the Indonesian film *The Raid* easily identifiable. However, I want to highlight the name of the story 'Scarlet'. In this issue, Scarlet is the name of a young girl that has been kidnapped as part of a dispute between two crime families. Mr Knight arrives at where she is located and battles his way, floor by floor, to rescue her. Mr Knight makes it clear he is not interested in the wider crimes the families may have committed, only that an innocent was kidnapped and should be returned.

However, this is not the first Scarlet that Moon Knight has crossed paths with. In issue #14 of volume 1, Moench introduced Scarlet Fasinera, a.k.a., Stained Glass Scarlet. Scarlet was a woman that renounced her vows as a nun to marry and have a son. However, her husband was a violent man affiliated with the mob and was killed by the police. This event drove her son to follow in his father's footsteps, quickly becoming known as Joe 'Mad Dog' Fasinera, because of the number of people he shot. By the time of the story, Joe has escaped from prison and is making his way to a church that Scarlet now calls home. Her only desire is to talk her son into giving himself up and changing his ways. However, when the final confrontation reaches its climax, Scarlet has shot her son dead.

The issue is another prime example of Moench's social commentary stories. In this case, he explores the idea of generational anger causing violence, the possibility of redemption and a strong anti-gun statement. Joe acts as the centre of this, having shot 6 men because of anger generated by nature and nurture. Is it possible to come back from that? Scarlet hopes he can.

The threat of gun violence weighs heavy throughout the issue, with all the deaths in the book a result of gun violence. In addition, Moench includes a sequence between Marc and Marlene, in which they touch on Marc's past as a mercenary and his current role as Moon Knight acting as his redemption. This is topped off with a panel in which Marlene sits at a piano and chooses to play "In my life" by The Beatles. Both Marc and Marlene cry, remembering that John Lennon was shot and killed less than a year before the release of the issue.

The choice of "in my life" is interesting. It was written by John Lennon, tying his real-world death to the gun violence of the story. However, the lyrics are also relevant, not just for Stained Glass Scarlet, but also for what Ellis is doing in his run.

For Scarlet, the final verse describes her story, of how she still loves those that have been in her life, and despite everything, she still wants the best for them:

> Though I know I'll never lose affection
> For people and things that went before
> I know I'll often stop and think about them
> In my life I love you more.[14]

For Ellis however, I suggest the opening verse highlights his desire to reference the past and show that what remains has evolved, and not always for the better. Both Moon Knight and the world he inhabits:

> There are places I'll remember
> All my life though some have changed
> Some forever, not for better
> Some have gone and some remain[15]

Returning to the changed Moon Knight, Mr Knight, while Moench introduced an anti-violence message, Ellis delivers a violent fight sequence that would make Jackie Chan wince. Not only is the violence brilliantly choreographed by Declan Shalvey, but it's also clear that Mr knight is revelling in it. Cracking jokes and even complimenting one combatant's style. This is not the Moon Knight that wept for the passing of John Lennon. This is a man on a mission and a man who loves that mission.

The Scarlet of Volume 1 was defined and damaged by her past and the mistakes she believed she had made. She cannot move on, returning to the church where she took her vows and got married. Unable to untangle herself from her past. The Ellis Scarlet is unphased by the events and even acknowledges Mr Knight's mask as his real face. This is a Scarlet that is adjusted to the world of violence and can move forward.

The final issue of the run is almost Moon Knight free, as it centres on Ryan Trent. A young New York police officer assigned to the 'freak beat', cleaning up after the superheroes. In this issue, Ellie pulls direct parallels with issue #25 of the original run, and the origin of Black Spectre, Carson Knowles.

Issue #25 works as another of Moench's social commentaries as it follows a Vietnam War soldier, Knowles returning home from the war to find everything

---

[14] "In My Life." The Beatles. *Rubber Soul*, 1965. Written by John Lennon and Paul McCartney.
[15] Ibid.

he knew had gone. His wife left, his job given to someone else, the connections his family had dried up, and the city he knew had moved on. These repeated humiliations are depicted in a montage culminating in Knowles taking out a mugger in anger and frustration. This is paralleled by Ellis in issue #5 as the reader is taken through Trent's life and the constant message that he isn't good enough, just a disappointment. His moment of frustration boil-over takes the reader back to issue #1. It is revealed that Trent was at the crime scene that opened the run. Seeing the police being given the brush off my Mr Knight is the final straw, now a freak is telling him he isn't good enough.

This is where the two men differ. Knowles becomes Black Spectre to spread fear and violence, so that, as Knowles, he can manipulate events to become Mayor of New York. He wants to control it all and be loved for it. Black Spectre is a means to an end. For Trent however, becoming the freak is the point. He doesn't want to destroy Moon Knight; he wants to replace him.

Knowles is a cautionary tale of gaining power as a way of revenge. He wants to hold a position of political power and influence. However, not an aspirational position, but one of corruption. This would be seen as an important and celebrated figure, the Mayor of one of the biggest cities in the world. Ellis, however, shows that Trent is a young man of the 21st century and his aspiration is not one of political power, but celebrity cache. He wants, what he sees as an easy way to be seen as special, to become Moon Knight.

In his journey to do so, Ellis pulls from the past in several other ways. There is the return of Marlene, now using Fontaine rather than Alraune, referring to the name used by Moench when she was first introduced in Marvel Spotlight #28 (1976). Also, Jean-Paul Duchamp, Frenchie. By introducing these in this last issue of the run Ellis confirms that Moon Knight has distanced himself from all elements of his past. We have not seen these characters, but the door was open a crack to let them back in. This short sequence closes that door, or at least closes it a little bit more.

This issue and run climaxes in Trent's failed attempt to kill Moon Knight with explosives. Trent is hit by a blast, left bloodied and broken while Mr Knight stands over him. Trent has confessed that he wants to be Moon Knight, be loved as he is, and that he is doing it as Black Spectre. Moon Knight considers this and responds "Let me tell you about Black Spectre. He really just wanted to be loved... Let me tell you a thing about me. People who love me suffer and die.

I never want to be loved. That's why I always win."[16] Ending on a note of isolation and distancing from the past, Moon Knight walks into his future.

In each of the issues in his run, Warren Ellis delivers a deconstruction of who Moon Knight was, and who he has become. With Marvel Now! Ellis and his creative team were able to acknowledge the past and shake it off. Examining slasher killers and military snipers dealing with abandoned, duty and family. The ghosts of pasts violence, whether supernatural or criminal. All the while creating a new Moon Knight. This run acted as a line in the sand and the runs that followed built on new ideas on the back of it. Moon Knight will always change a little under the pen of each creative team, but it was Ellis's run that cut the strings and created an attitude that has remained.

---

[16] "Spectre." *Moon Knight* Vol. 7 #6 (2014). By Warren Ellis, Declan Shalvey, and Jordie Belaire.

Shooting for the Moon

by Matt Corrigan

Crescent Crusader. Lunar Légionnaire. Moony. Moon Man. Fist of Khonshu. Moon Knight is a superhero known by many names. The thing is, not every comic book fan knows them, knows *him*. After reading a few of his books you can see he's actually a pretty heavy hitter in the Marvel Universe. He's held his own not just on the page but in a medium where new spandex heroes pop up (land in spaceships or get irradiated) every day, and old ones fade away or get the axe just as quickly. Yet since his inception in 1975, in *Werewolf by Night* Vol. 1 issue #32, Moon Knight has been a constant but often overlooked Marvel character. He's had multiple titles of his own, as well as appearances in other characters' books and events, sometimes in a pivotal role. Despite this Moon Knight has remained, at most, a C-list character; comic readers may have heard of him and seen him in an issue of so-and-so, but he's a character most never really read, and frankly don't know much about. It's time to shed some light on what makes this character so intriguing but also examine why many comic book fans have left him in the dark. Lucky for us, there's a Hunter's Moon tonight...

From his earliest incarnation, courtesy of Don Perlin to the tattered cape David Finch shrouded him in and beyond, the look of Moon Knight is just and has always been, *badass*! The aesthetic design of the character is one of the most captivating parts of his appeal. The contrast between the oft-referenced jet and silver is visually striking. It makes the hero look bright and shining, while at the same time allowing him to live in the shadows. Every version of his costume hides his face, completely, creating an air of mystery that entices the reader to want to know more, even if we know who is under the mask (and let's face it, with this character, even that's up in the air).

Let's talk a little about that mask... It can be downright spooky. We can often see the shape of the face of the man underneath: his brow, his eye sockets, his nose, and many times his open mouth. This is usually depicted when our hero is in distress, and it looks like he can't escape the costume itself. It's terrifying. For the audience, this image can invoke the feeling of not being able to breathe, as if a bag were over their head. The taught mask pulled tight against his face contorts it to a ghastly, almost inhuman image, much like a mummy or some EC Comics ghoul.

Another aspect of Moon Knight's costume appreciated by his fans is how incredible it looks when it's all torn up. The only way to make that uniform look more striking is to run it through the mud and dirt, rip it up and poke a ton of holes in the cape and hood. Add a little crimson blood to that stark white palette and it puts Moon Knight's look over the top. He just looks so *awesome* all beat up. The through-the-wringer look is something that many superheroes don at some point. Be it when Spider-Man smashes or loses an eye lens, or when the Dark Knight is returning triumphant despite his slashed suit and bruised face, the tattered appearance of their costumes adds a depth that's more than cloth-deep.

It might not work for all costumed characters, but we readers like it for more than just the way it changes a character's familiar appearance. When we see a hero that looks like he was just hit by a truck (and sometimes that's the case) we have an inherent urge to root for them. When we're seeing them at their worst (bloody, bruised, their colours and emblems battered and torn) we realize there's only one way for them to go: up. They are about to rise above, overcome, and conquer. This of course applies to our man Moon Knight. He rarely fights beings as powerful as Galactus, but his adversaries can dish out a beating. A beating Moon Knight will take, then get back up and give as good as he just got. The visual representation of the hardship the character has endured is a storytelling element that does more than just make the character *look cool*. Let's be honest though, some characters do look so striking, all beaten up. In addition to the ones already mentioned, I'd certainly put Daredevil and Punisher on that list, as well as Invincible and (now this is important) Wolverine. Can you think of a character that looks better covered in blood, wearing the torn rags of what used to be a bright costume, the holes in his suit revealing wounds that won't even slow him down? It's almost weird to see Wolverine in a spotless costume.

Now here's why it's important: this too is a subtle message to the reader. Not only does a mutilated costume prepare the audience for their hero's ascension to victory, but in many cases, it is also a testament to the punishment the character can endure. It signifies how tough the hero is, and how much pain they can take. The more damage to the costume, the more damage to the hero. The more damage to the hero, the stronger they must be, and the more monumental (and satisfying) their comeback will be. So, when they're posing in a full-page splash in a mangled costume, ready to take on the villain, we're gnashing our teeth along with them, because they are badass. Every single patch and piece of medical tape on *Sin City*'s Marv's face is a warning, saying "Don't f*** with me. This didn't stop me, and you won't either."

When we see Moon Knight's costume barely hanging on him, making him, even more, wraith-like than normal, we are excited about whatever he's about to surmount. His torn shroud is a testament to how tough he is. We know he will never give up, he's way too tenacious. He may never come upon a force that can keep him down (and his fans know not even death has stopped him yet).

Maybe part of the reason we love Moon Knight's costume all shredded up is that the costume, as a whole, looks like something that could be homemade. It's believable. Peter Parker made his Spider-Man costume at home. This may be a little far-fetched, but hey, it's a comic book so we allow it. He *also* made his own web shooters. Scratch that. He *invented* them! Again, we accept this because of the fantastic medium Spidey lives in. Moon Knight though... he's a little more *bare-bones*. After his first few appearances in *Werewolf by Night*, he drops most of the actual silver from his costume and weapons. Sometimes donning a bit of armour, always with his white uniform, mask, and cloak... this seems like a costume someone in the real world could have. The same is true for many of his weapons. While embedded grappling hooks aren't readily available in our world, a lot of Moon Knight's arsenal is: truncheon, nunchucks, and crescent darts. Now, of course, he does have multiple fancy helicopters, but his character has the bankroll to back that idea up. As a young adult, Spider-Man / Peter Parker must peddle photos "to stay in web fluid." Steven Grant is rich, so we can believe he owns a private helicopter, and because he lives in a comic book, we can suspend disbelief enough to accept his fortune could help him develop futuristic airships.

David Finch's original art of the tattered and bloodied hero, from the writer's personal collection.

Speaking of comic books, in his debut Moon Knight takes on a werewolf for two issues. Even the cover of *Werewolf by Night* #32 depicts the Lunar Avenger pummeling the beast so ferociously that it looks like he's about to knock him off the page. Werewolf by Night is *afraid* of this brutal, fearless, unrelenting fighter. This man, this mercenary, is hired by the Committee to capture a super-strong ruthless beast and does so easily. He delivers the werewolf to the Committee, but quickly changes allegiances and frees the *monster* when he sees it fights only for its freedom. He even taunts the Committee with "That's the kind of fight I support, lard-butts!!"[1] This immature quip proves how unconcerned he is with the situation, it's not a big deal to him. Why? Because he has already held his own against a lycanthrope and being in the same room with it while it tears through a bunch of fat cats in suits is possibly his idea of a good time. When the dust settles, it's unclear how many Committee members are dead because of the werewolf, and how many Moon Knight may have killed. The answer is probably more than zero.

Marc Spector is a mercenary, with training and experience in ending lives. And, as we eventually find out, he has not been all that discriminating about the lives he ends. Does this street-level hero have powers? It's often left to the reader to decide. He may have quicker reflexes and instincts from a werewolf bite, and he also believes that as the servant of Khonshu, he receives power from the moon. All that said though, we're not talking about the strength to lift cars or leap tall buildings. Yet Moon Knight appears to have the agility of Spider-Man. His creators and artists often draw him in elaborate flips and poses that we're accustomed to seeing from the wall crawler. He's an Olympic-level athlete who seems just as confident fighting an armed gang as he is when fighting a supernatural beast.

Unlike Spidey, though, who ultimately seems to not want to hurt anyone, Moon Knight's fighting style is brutal. Like Daredevil, Moon Knight often dispatches his enemies with a club. There's no gentle way to take someone down with a club, and Moon Knight doesn't seem too worried about hurting people. A point exemplified in *Moon Knight* Vol. 4 #7, when he smashes a disarmed thug with a wooden board... in front of Spider-Man. I wouldn't call Spider-Man *violent*, but it is a term I would use for Moon Knight. This can be

---

[1] "Wolf-Beast vs. Moon Knight." *Werewolf by Night* Vol. 1 #33 (1975). By Doug Moench, Gil Kane, and Phil Rache.

traced back to his origins. He has been called the *moon's avenger*. The word "avenge" means to exact vengeance, which in turn is usually driven by anger. That emotion is often the force that drives Moon Knight. Many of his physical fights are described in the third person, informing readers how mad an enemy has made him, and how his actions are dictated by his fury. Forget the actual Avengers! Moon Knight is a *literal* avenger, violently smashing down evil... with a stick!

Peeling back another layer of the cowl we can see the savageness goes beyond our hero's actions. Moon Knight is not simply a violent fighter. He truly is an unbalanced, ruthless person. Let's put the possibility of Moon Knight having Dissociative Identity Order (DID) aside, as well as all the behavioural ramifications that could be tied to that disorder (that's a big ask, but, come on, we read books about a guy who floats down from a sci-fi helicopter using only his cape). Moon Knight, as a *hero,* has done some very questionable things, and we know he is comfortable in a cracked mindset. Of Midnight Man Moon Knight states, "I rather liked the man... he was... refreshingly psychotic."[2] But that's just the tip of the iceberg. In *Moon Knight* Vol. 1 #10, after defeating Bushman in a flooding chamber Moon Knight tells some cops to "grab this guy before he drowns" as he stands over his foe's unconscious body which is lying face-down in the rising water. Was Moon Knight not going to pick Bushman up? Is his moral code so blurred that he'd let a stunned enemy drown at his feet? Let's face it: the world's not black and white (not even the four-coloured world of comics) but that is one mighty large grey area.

Moon Knight is the jet and silver avenger and, despite there being so much white on his uniform, there is a lot of darkness within him. This is a man, a superhero, who spat on a terrorist he knocked out after foiling his plans to bomb New York City (*Moon Knight* Vol. 1 #20). Can you imagine Spider-Man spitting on a foe? Iron Man? Captain Ameri... no, I can't even write that, not even as a hypothetical. A fully functioning member of society doesn't spit on another person. A superhero should be held to at least the same level as the average person when it comes to that ethical standard, right? We can deduce that this lunar warrior is therefore a bit unhinged. This malleable or even broken code of what's right and wrong doesn't necessarily make Moon Knight

---

[2] "Midnight Means Murder." *Moon Knight* Vol. 1 #3 (1980). By Doug Moench, Bill Sienkiewicz, and Bob Sharen.

cool (although to many readers, and 90s comics, it may), however, it does make him more interesting, more intriguing, and certainly adds a lot of depth.

So, we have this lunar avenger, an ex-killer with a moral code that is often hard to pin down. He has multiple identities that may or may not be a mental illness, which may or may not destabilize his reality. This leaves him with a past so mysterious even he isn't sure of his true origin story. He's garbed in an incredibly slick-looking costume, complete with a cape shaped like his namesake, which looks dynamite against the night sky. He fights with an arsenal of varied weapons and vehicles, from basic to fantastic, most brutal, and some lethal. He's tough as nails and can take a beating, and when he does, he looks even more imposing with his slashed costume and a dirty, torn cape full of holes. He can dish out even more pain than he can soak up and his violence is not discerning, taking on the mafia one night, ending a serial killer's massacre the next, and then fighting a werewolf over the weekend.

So why hasn't Moon Knight ever broken into the A-list of superherodom? Is there a glass (or Vibranium) ceiling over the C-list that even spiked gauntlets and helicopters can't get through? Or maybe it's that Moon Knight has the *gadgets* but not the *tools* to break through.

One thing, and perhaps the biggest, is that Moon Knight is missing a formidable foe, a worthy arch-nemesis. Sure, he has Raoul Bushman, but is he a nemesis? A yin to Spector's yang? A Joker to his Batman, or a Green Goblin to his Spider-Man? Bushman has been an effective villain, and the two characters' hatred for each other is fun and interesting to explore, but he can't hold the title of Moon Knight's rival. He's not a constant enough threat, and he's not a big enough menace. For a superhero nemesis to work, the villain needs to be a tangible threat, to both the hero and what and whom the hero holds dear. The hero needs to be a bit afraid of the nemesis, or at least unsure of victory. The Jester isn't Daredevil's nemesis because before we open that issue, we know who's going to win. Bullseye, on the other hand, has murdered more than one of Matt Murdock's girlfriends and is outright deadly. He also *knows* Murdock and not just his identity. He knows how to push DD's buttons, and how to get under his skin. Those characters hate each other, to the point where, when Bullseye is lying bloodied at Daredevil's feet, the reader will be concerned that this is the time Daredevil snaps and finishes his maniacal foe off for good. That's a nemesis. You truly don't know who will win in that scenario. Even though you may think Daredevil is the better fighter and will triumph in the battle, Bullseye gets his hooks into him so deep and may push him so far that Daredevil snaps, making it Bullseye's victory even if he lost the physical fight. Nemesis! Charlie Huston's take on Moon Knight tried to have a few characters rise to the nemesis challenge, but without the history and substance to back it up the rivalries in those books felt kind of empty. The fights were full of rancour and spite, but only on a surface level.

So, Moon Knight might not have a good enough nemesis to consistently clash with, but at least he's got some interesting baddies to fight, right? He's got a decent rogues gallery, doesn't he? Well... how many can you name? Even if you could name a few, would you say they were interesting or memorable? I've read a bunch of Moon Knight books, both over the years as a fan and also specifically to write this piece, and I *still* had to look up Moon Knight's rogues' gallery. Even then I *still* didn't recognize more than half the names mentioned, and the recognizable names weren't even B-list. We're talking about the panel-filling characters for events like Marvel's *Civil War*.

It's often said, and specifically about comics, that a hero is only as good as his villains. Moon Knight just doesn't have a decent rogues gallery. They're not so much *villains* as they are *fill-ins*. He's such an interesting character with so much going for him, but let's just say he's got no Bullseyes and a lot of Jesters. His villains don't even have the branding of Jester. That's not to say he has no decent villains or hasn't entered into any interesting conflicts or confrontations. However, he lacks frequently occurring adversaries with any real staying power. Even those who do pop up from time to time are of little consequence, both to Moon Knight and the Marvel Universe at large.

That said, *why* doesn't Moon Knight have any challenging rivals? It can be suggested that it has more to do with Moon Knight's foundational makeup than a lack of creativity on the part of the artists and writers. Moon Knight gets his power from the moon, or so he believes. He was resurrected, multiple times...maybe. A warrior priest of a deity, he has been bequeathed with abilities and power greater than that of a normal man...or not. You see, Moon Knight himself isn't even sure of his potential, nor where it came from. The writers and artists who have worked on him usually use that to their (and the story's) advantage, not taking a firm stance either way. This boils down to the fact that Moon Knight may or may not have supernatural skills. That is, he may or may not have superpowers. While this is a fascinating character trait for a superhero, it kind of makes it hard to create a villain for him to clash with. Should the villain have powers? If so, to what extent? You obviously can't create a competitor that's way more powerful than the hero, nor can you make him significantly less powerful. The power sets should be comparable so that the stakes are not just fair but, more importantly, the outcome is undetermined at the beginning of the conflict, thus creating suspense. This is very important when creating an arch-nemesis. A good arch-nemesis should be a corrupt version of the hero. He should be as similar to the protagonist as possible, with only one or two really momentous (and often symbolic) differences. This not only puts them at odds but keeps them from being almost the same character. Professor X and Magneto are great examples. They want *almost* the same thing, it means a great deal to them both, but they go about it in very different ways. A good arch-nemesis is what the hero is afraid he'll see when he looks in the mirror. Yet a problem arises when you have a comic book hero that *might* have superpowers. You can't make a villain who also *might* have powers. Even if Moon Knight does have powers, they're not clearly defined or quantifiable. So how do you assemble a direct foil using those vague parameters? Who is Moon Knight afraid to see when he looks in the mirror? Marc Spector may be the best answer to that question, and while that might make for a good story or character evolution, it doesn't work as an arch-nemesis.

A bit confusing? Some people think so, and this might be another factor barring the gate to Moon Knight's ascension to the big time. Many of the traits of this character are a bit confusing. Readers enjoy comic books as an escape. They read comics because heroism and villainy are usually easily defined and although the conflicts are bigger than life, they are easy to grasp. Even when the issues in the story are a bit more complex, following along and understanding them usually isn't. Enter a figure who may or may not have superpowers. A champion who has multiple origins, some supernatural and some not, with a few redirecting retcons. And although he's one man, he's got four different personas, or is it personalities? Is there even a difference in this case? Some readers may be turned off by Moon Knight's muddy dossier.

Almost every other superhero has a clearly defined list of powers and weaknesses and usually, at most, one single alternate (and/or secret) identity. This becomes extremely important when we're talking about a character with his own title.

Having your own book is like pulling your fandom aboard a ship you're captaining. That ship has to be a vessel in and of itself and needs a little direction. Those sailing with Moon Knight are on a craft whose ability is unknown and have no idea who is even at the wheel. The problem of Moon Knight not having a clear power set goes beyond making it difficult to create interesting villains for him to face off against. It means the reader doesn't know what to expect from their protagonist at any given moment. Is he taking down a mob or a cult? Perhaps a bit far-fetched but still believable and grounded. Or is he a true superhero with extra abilities who can and will have a showdown with a super-powered villain? If the latter, does he have super strength? Super-speed? Just generally tougher than the average Joe? In a tense scene from Jed Mackay's take on the character, Moon Knight sits comfortably, even casually as he reminds a bar full of supervillains surrounding him that no one in the room, not even he, knows what he's capable of.[3] While this makes for a cool, action movie one-liner, it can also leave readers and fans wanting. Moon Knight's power set is a bit of a mystery, making it hard for fans to relate to, comprehend, and enjoy his adventures. Oh, and those powers, vague as they may be, are suggested to be dependent on the phases of the moon? Most people aren't all that familiar with the phases of the moon. We know what a spider can do, sure. We understand losing one sense and having the remaining senses heightened. But I have no clue how or when or what the moon does. Does Moon Knight know? Does Marc Spector? How about Jake Lockley or Steven Grant? Whose powers are we even debating here?

The many faces beneath Moon Knight's mask also make it a bit arduous at times to get on his (their?) bandwagon. I know that I, personally, wasn't into Moon Knight books for quite a while specifically because of the whole *multiple-personality* aspect of them. It's a big pill to swallow. Most superheroes have a secret identity they use to shield their personal life from the dangers and threats of their hero life. This is not just a logical and simple concept, it's also fun. Who doesn't wish they could be someone else, even if just once in a while, even if just for a short period? It's a very important trope of the superhero. Yet with Moon Knight, it becomes a whole other beast. He doesn't just use a non-super-hero identity as a cover, to keep his costumed life separate from his personal life. His personal lives, and his non-costumed personas, are part of his heroic life and are incredibly important to the actual make-up of Moon Knight as its / his own separate identity.

Hard to keep straight, especially if we look at each persona/personality. Mercenary Marc Spector is arguably the first and true identity of Moon Knight.

---

[3] "Headhunters." *Moon Knight* Vol. 10 #7 (2022). By Jed MacKay, Federico Sabbatini, and Rachelle Rosenburg.

Most origins feature Spector as a killer-for-hire, good at violence and bad at morals. It's easy to imagine a superhero whose backstory is that he used to be a hired gun, now fighting crime as an act of redemption. Makes sense, is interesting, and certainly fits the hero mould. He could be Moon Knight when the sun goes down, using the funds the mercenary had accumulated to do costumed good, then resuming life as Marc Spector during the day. Many aspects of this hypothetical are part of the published Moon Knight character's backstory. Yet Moon Knight's identities make this streamlined concept three times as intricate.

Presumably, Spector is so ashamed of who he is/was that he doesn't want to be that person anymore, at least not all the time. So, he creates/becomes Steven Grant, an immensely wealthy man, similar to Bruce Wayne, as the means to finance Moon Knight's mission. Oh, but that's not all. Moon Knight *also* needs a man on the street... and that, for some reason, also needs to be him, not a friend or someone he can hire. Enter Jake Lockley, a man with access to information no one else has because he drives a cab. Really? Even in the '70s and '80s, were New York taxi drivers an unparalleled hub for information on the underhanded? I don't recall Gotham cabbies being badgered by Batman too often... Couldn't the Spector identity do the same job as Jake? I mean, with all the special forces training and experience he (Spector) had, I figure he could handle recon and information gathering. Even so, that leaves us with two personas in addition to the costumed one. That's a lot for a reader to follow. Also, if that's not enough, allies like Marlene, Frenchie, Crawley, Gena, Ray, and Ricky Landers all call Moon Knight different/multiple names, in addition to making some of his personas redundant. It's not hard to imagine a reader, especially a kid, putting this book down to read instead about *one* guy who flies around in an armoured robot suit.

This doesn't mean you need a degree in psychology to understand or even enjoy Moon Knight, but it does make it harder to wrap your head around the character. The remainder of his mythos doesn't make Moon Knight any more accessible either. The character, his origins, and his *powers* have a subtle yet constant undercurrent of religion. Moon Knight is quite possibly the avatar of Khonshu, an ancient Egyptian god of the moon. Have you ever seen a line for the comic con panel about Egyptian religion and how it relates to the contemporary superhero? No? There's a reason for that. Even if that panel did exist, many comic book readers would probably look for a more exciting panel to spend their time on. The same is true for the comics and characters they're drawn to on the newsstand.

On top of that, religion, in general, has the potential to be a controversial, hot-button topic. Most entertainment media will avoid it wherever possible. Yet Moon Knight dives out of his crescent copter, headfirst into this taboo motif. And he hits every fire escape on the way down, as the religious themes in the Moon Knight titles aren't clearly illustrated. Through the years of Moon Knight's career, Khonshu has been revealed to be the God of Vengeance as well as the Shepherd of the Lost. Ok, but supposedly Khonsu is *also* the protector of travellers in the night. What? Seems like the only thing this deity isn't worshipped for is picking a thematic lane. And while most Moon Knight books don't delve too deep into the religious aspect of the character, the more recent adventures of the hero don't shy away either.

Khonshu him/itself has become his own character, more and more intertwined with Moon Knight himself. While at first simply a statue that Moon Knight revered, Khonshu has since become an animate devil on the superhero's shoulder. Taunting and goading him into action, causing him the self-doubt and inner strife many readers like their comic book protagonists to endure. The spectre has also become a constant and visual reminder to both the reader and Moon Knight himself that there might be an otherworldly, interdimensional being behind Moon Knight's power and his thirst for violence. Spurring his actions, manipulating him for its own ends which may or may not be nefarious. Or Marc Spector may just be crazy and hallucinating. Warren Ellis' slick run dabbled with merging *both* those options: what if Khonshu, an interdimensional being, was an actual entity that exacerbated Marc's very real mental illness? Whether Khonshu is the coping strategy of an imbalanced man or Moon Knight is the warrior priest of an imbalanced god, is it any wonder this West Coast Avenger hasn't made it into any Saturday morning cartoons?

Hero. Murderer. A sufferer of mental illness. Moon Knight may be all these and more, but one thing he is not is A-list. Regardless of whether they think he's a *badass* crusader fighting the good fight after being resurrected and given powers by an Egyptian God, or just an average man with a mental health condition, comic book fandom has chosen to leave Moon Knight on the C-list... for now. As of this writing, the new Moon Knight show on Disney+ hasn't premiered yet. Could it be the springboard needed to propel this character into the spotlight? Or will he stick to the shadows of comic book fandom like he always has done? Would Moon Knight be at home on the top tier of superherodom? Can he even exist that way, or would becoming a household name change the very essence of who the character is? The show will be the next phase of Moon Knight. Whether it (and he) succeeds or fails, it's probably safe to say that Frenchie will still drop the rope ladder down to whisk Moon Knight away to his next adventure. The question is: will we all be with him?

Bill Sienkiewicz
Interview

Bill Sienkiewicz entered the comic industry with Moon Knight in the HULK! Magazine, influencing the design and style of the comic for many years. He went on to become one of the most distinctive comic book artists in the industry, developing his style in New Mutants, Elektra: Assassin, Daredevil: Love and War, and The Shadow. He has won numerous awards for his art and contributions to the comic book industry. This interview was conducted on 26th January 2022.

Scott Weatherly (SW): How did you get brought on to draw Moon Knight, as the backup for Hulk magazine?

Bill Sienkiewicz (BS): That was a completely strange turn of events. I had never really heard of the character at the time. To compress it as much as I can, I always wanted to do comic books. I loved comics, I always felt like they chose me, you know, that feeling of doing them for a career. I had drawn them all through high school for myself. Then I went to art school, and my friends were graduating, I hung out with the older students and said well I've always wanted to do comics let me put together a portfolio, but I didn't think my work was good enough for Marvel. Neal Adams was an influence when I was younger, so I said well, let me dive back into the Neal Adams thing. I did, I don't know, about 15 pages of artwork, with all of Neal's characters, all the DC characters, and I took the train from new jersey into New York. This was in the era when you could walk into a reception area and just sit down on a couch and you didn't need any form of ID, a blood sample or DNA. I just sat down, and they took pity on me. Vinny Coletta, the inker, was the art director at DC at the time, said "We could use you…" this was during the time of the DC implosion, "but you'll be out on the street again in about six weeks, I'm going to do you a favour and I'm going to call up Neal Adams". So, he called up Neal Adams, and you know, I'm in my pants you could play chess on, just like little Abner. So, I went to meet Neal and Neal called up Jim Shooter at Marvel. So, I ended up going to Marvel and getting hired.

I was hoping to get a review of my portfolio, they would say "Look you're not quite ready, come back in a year, come back in two years or give it up completely", it was the whole gamut. Never in my wildest imaginings did I think I'd get a career out of it, you know, let alone a career at Marvel with nothing but DC characters.

Shooter looked at it and everybody who looked at the work said, obviously you would be perfect for Batman. I could see them off in the distance sort of talking to each other and they said, "We want to give you this character called Moon Knight". I guess they thought that was a character that was more Batman like. So, I had no idea who it was, but they told me it was going to be in the backup of Hulk Magazine, coloured by Steve Oliff, and it was his first professional gig as well. We started on the same one, and then of course I was really fortunate to have Joe Rubenstein ink me, and it was right out the gate I went from "Oh, I hope they won't kick me out" to, here's a career, here's a character. So that was sort of the genesis of how I started working on Moon Knight. I know they had made him have a moral code, they had made him a good guy in the Werewolf by Night stuff, sort of, teaming up with the protagonist, although he was the antagonist, you know, that's the abbreviated version of how I came to be involved.

SW: It's amazing, just taking the chance and where it took you. You mention your style when you came in, and obviously, it's been compared to Neal Adams. Was that a conscious choice then when you started, did you think "Oh that's the comic style" or more of a conscious choice?

BS: At that point it was. I sort of felt he was a super big influence on me, on my work during high school and my younger days. Then when I went to art school I started finding out about illustration, fine art, and abstract expressionism, I mean everything, plus music, Jazz. I just sort of realised I was the guts, mind, and constitution of an artist, you know. As much as I loved comics, everything else I was enamoured of and enamoured by was something I wanted to see if I could fit into comics. I wanted comics to be able to handle anything, I felt like they could. So, at that point, when I went in to start working at Marvel, it was kind of a conscious decision to emulate Neal because it was familiar and it was comfortable to people, and there were a number of people that got into the business emulating him. It wasn't until more than halfway through the run when the criticisms about my work were saying I was just a clone, meanwhile, my sketchbooks were full of all these other things that my work eventually became. It wasn't until I think Morpheus and Black Spectre, around issue 21, and then when I plotted 'Hit it' because that was where I felt I wanted to go with it, with the character. Then I think the last ten issues was when we really hit our stride, you know, in terms of making it all click. But it was a conscious decision and was as much of a conscious decision to say that I'm either going to do the character and comics my way or I'm going to get out because I felt the clone moniker was starting to ware very thin.

SW: I can imagine. I mean you say about those issues, and it's evident, I mean I've read your work across that initial run and it's clear, your panel layouts become more inventive, and 'Hit it' is a fantastic issue. I love the way the music thrums throughout the issue, but also you mention Jack Russell and obviously, the werewolf comes back and, as you mention, the design of Morpheus is great. When you were doing that, you were being looser and more relaxed, but were there any other influences coming through, were there things influencing you at the time, or was it just you wanting to try new things?

BS: Yeah, there were. At the time I started getting into painting and so there were a number of illustrators at the time that were very popular. Contemporary illustrators, and artists like Bob Peak who did the Superman Movie poster, Apocalypse Now, he was a big influence on my work. Bernie Fuchs, another illustrator, was terrific. There was a whole American school of illustration, plus there were children's book illustrators that I really got into. Animation as well. These things sort of percolated. Like Tex Avery and Chuck Jones sort of became an influence when I went on to do the 'Love and War' graphic novel, with The King Pin. But it was hard to just pick one thing that was influencing me at the time I started breaking away in terms of Moon Knight. It was like pushing all this stuff through a sieve. It was wide open and at the same time I realised I had to tell the story that the character had, what they were going through. So, it wasn't too many other comic book artists that were influencing me it was more from outside. Some advertising campaign stuff that felt very noncomic book. A certain feeling, I got from people, even my, well ex-wide now, saying "That's not what comics are, you can't put that in comics". I would get that from people in the business as well, but luckily, I had editors like Ralph Macchio and others that were excited about these things.

SW: I always love that, when you hear in history someone being told you can't do that, and so they do it and is really impressive. You set the mould for many of these characters, Marc, Marlene and Frenchie in particular, but then also so many others. When you were first starting to draw them and you were choosing how to depict them, were there real people in your life, and you were like, that's the Marlene or that's the Marc or anything like that?

BS: Interesting. I think, looking back at it now, the one thing, that I do not necessarily regret, but because I was so steeped in the Neal Adams vain, I felt like everything sort of had his imprinting on it. Some of my decisions, my choices, and when I decided to break away from that style he was as much of an influence in the reverse. It was going from, I want to draw like Neal to Neal factored in where I wanted to do things, not like him, but he was still in the equation. I was running away from that as opposed to doing what was called for in the story.

I had a lot of fun with characters like Crawley and the ancillary characters. The character of Marlene, I do realise she was somewhat influenced by Stan Drake's take on Eve Jones in *The Heart of Juliet Jones*, the blonde, because Stan was another big influence, but he was one removed from Neal Adams. If I was to do it now, I think, ... it's a what-if scenario I play through my head sometimes, if the Neal Adams influence hadn't been so strong what would I have done? How would I have seen them? The fact they are doing the series now, and Jake Lockley's a cab driver, I haven't seen a cab in Manhattan unless he's now an Uber Driver.

SW: Talking about Jake, Doug Moench said in the past that he always saw Jake, Steven Grant, and Marc Spector as disguises. They have developed over time but when you were drawing each of them did you have key aspects you used to differentiate them, and did you have a favourite one of them to draw?

BS: Well, I think the idea of him having multiple disguises, in a weird way, I felt the disguises aspect somehow didn't quite sit with me, the way I think it did with Doug. I was always a big proponent of mental health, and I thought in the back of my mind someone who would do all that, even if they were disguises, it was a lot of work to go through all those disguises. I mean if he's going to be a millionaire playboy like Bruce Wayne and then do all these others, especially if he's also a mercenary as well. There were certain things I tried to do to make them somewhat separate, I think I gave Jake a toothpick and there was a costume he kind of wore, so to speak, with the cap you know. For Marc, I kept thinking of Clint Eastwood when I was drawing him, and I was trying not to think of Bruce Wayne when I was thinking of Steven. It was like not thinking about the Polar bear, don't think of Bruce Wayne, don't think of Batman, he's his own character. So yeah, there was that aspect of it. It's so interesting revisiting this.

SW: You talk about the toothpick, and I do like some of the differentiators like the cockiness of Jake Lockley is fun, on the flip side though you also go to design some cool villains, like Morpheus. Stain Glass Scarlet is a favourite of mine, and as you were drawing Jack Russell as a werewolf, did you have fun designing these? Was Marvel a little looser with the designs because they weren't the hero?

BS: Yeah, I was having quite a bit of fun. I adore Denny O'Neal and I remember I would cut loose on the covers. We had this running joke; I think even in one of the issues I wrote a 2 or 3 page pictorial essay of different covers rejected by Denny. I was trying some of the things I would go on to do later, and I think Denny particularly felt they weren't comic book covers. I think I had eventually worn him down by issue twenty. I think Scarlet was fun for me because I adore that era of film, you know the "I'm ready for my close up Mr DeMille" kind of vintage aspect of it.

I think grounding the characters in more of a unique reality, one that wasn't, you know, because of all the associations with Moon Knight being Marvel's version of Batman. We didn't have a Joker, maybe Bushman. I felt like I would have liked to have pushed him even further, even more into sort of a grotesque. If somebody is going to get to that level of mercenary work or whatever, I feel I played it a bit safer than I would have liked to. Again, with Jack Russell, at that point, I think *The Howling* had come out and the werewolf had that elongated feeling, as opposed to that more compact Lon Chaney type, or what had been done in *Werewolf by Night*. So I was, for the time, bringing more modern influences from film and other areas.

I had so much fun doing the werewolf issue and again Scarlett because there were certain things, I was starting to see in real life, that made their way into Moon Knight. There are a couple of panels and scenes in the Stained Glass Scarlet story where you see trestles and you're underground, and I think there are some weird croppings of concrete and bridge work and things like that. I remember when I would take the train in when I would go to certain parts of

Manhattan, and you go underground you would see these flashes of light and dark, through tunnels, there were big slabs of concrete supporting the buildings above and yet you would see along the side of the train tracks, like a wire fence and places homeless people could live. It just felt like you were entering this darker portal. I started to become more influenced by what I was seeing in real life in terms of New York City, and aspects of the everyday. They evoked a very dark and gritty realism, it wasn't something I had seen in comics before but there were minor little adjustments and things that fascinated me, that I felt added to the grittiness of the character, and some of these things were really enjoyable to do.

SW: The Scarlet Issues are a favourite of mine, you mention that classic period with Marlene Dietrich and Lauren Bacall, she has that kind of feel. When you were doing these designs were there any you put forward that people said, "Oh that's too far or you can't do that", or caused a bit of controversy with the editors or Doug?

BS: The one I can think of is the Dieter Braun thing we mention before recording, drawing rats in little uniforms, that was a challenge, but not for any political reason more for putting them in little helmets and making it work. It was challenging for me as a young artist, but I would like to have pushed things more, that's the feeling I keep coming away with. I thought the character of [Black] Spectre, I think with the Knight look, the armoured helmet, just as dark in some respects and gritty as Moon Knight was, but with these glints of light off this black armour. That was the other thing that struck me. I really started to enjoy the graphic quality of the storytelling. Ideally, I felt like, the character was this black and white character, in terms of his costume and I thought if I was going into a comic shop and there would be this basked-in colour display, and I thought why not do some of these covers in black and white, as opposed to doing everything in colour? That's when Denny agreed I could do every other cover in black and white, with spatter and be very graphic. To me, it felt truer to the character, because the character was still defining himself to me, even though it was a one character book it was as much as doing the avengers or The Teen Titans, you know it was like a cast of twelve characters, plus the three that he had in himself. The idea of playing with the graphic approach and the dark, not full-blown colour to complete, this isn't the Teen Titans this isn't the X-men, this is its own thing.

Again, back when I did 'hit it', to me that sort of solidified how I felt about the character, but also how I felt about comics and music, and how it could move people in other ways. What would be the psychology of this character that has three other identities? It was also, at the time, reflecting on how I felt about my growing up and some of the violence I experienced, which were just aberrations of, I think, people's lives at one point or another. That people have weird things happen to them, but the idea I was getting into comic books, and I thought the idea of a character who is just a character, who in the story, wasn't particularly superheroic, didn't have a cape but was someone that was just very damaged. So, the idea came to me that you can either take stuff that has happened to you, and you can pay it forward with violence, or you can try and do something creative. That's why it was set to music. You think of so many of the musicians you know, Jazz musicians, and certainly the devil at the crossroads kind of performers and selling your soul. They are trying to make music out of something very dark. So, to me, I felt like 'go towards the light'. That was to do with that issue of Moon Knight, exploring characters that may not have been the caped villain of the month, but dealing with some larger issues. Then, of course, a couple of issues later we get into the werewolf by night, and it's like 'Hey, I get to do werewolves, and that's fun too.'.

SW: Yeah, you get to do both ends of the spectrum. Just to go back, I want to compliment those covers. Issue #25 in particular, Moon Knight coming through a channel, and you have Black Spectre lurching above him. It's one of the first issues I remember picking up. It's so incredibly striking and it stands out from the other garish covers but graphically, it's a statement. I have heard of the Marvel style, which I understand was prevalent at the time. Was Moon Knight done using the Marvel style, or were you handed a complete script, was there a discussion between you and Doug about panel layouts and other things?

BS: When I first came in, they gave me full scripts from Doug, and I think I bristled at that, because I realised that, as time went on, I'm a collaborator who wants to feel like I'm not just a set of hands. I don't like having all my decisions made for me, or sort of being dictated to. I drew and wrote my comics when I was growing up, so I had the idea of wanting to be a little more invested and involved and I think Doug and I found a way to work together when he allowed me greater freedom in terms of plotting. I remember having a conversation with him, I said "Tell me where you want me to get from and to, and I will do it but let me do it my way. Don't give me the whole panel layout, just give me the beats, and let me play with it", that felt more inviting to me than 'panel three, its down shot of ...' I would glaze over and I'm going to draw anything but that, it's the rebelliousness creeping in. In addition to the whole Neal Adams clone thing, I was probably sitting on quite a bit of volatile creativity and anger. So, it was like, don't tell me what to draw, just let me play, just put me in the game coach.

SW: It's one of those things I hear a lot, and it's cool to hear you had that collaboration and that sort of teamwork. You're an artist, that's what you're trusted to do, that is your job. You do the words and I'll interpret them through the artistic lens.

BS: Well, in some respects, I think Doug was saddled, I feel, with the newbie me. He was probably instructed on one level. Doug is such a wonderful writer. I mean I grew up on his work, so to work with him was a dream come true, but I also felt that he was also saddled with having to bring this quote Neal Adams clone along and try to find something that made it work for him as well. As I said, we hit our stride towards the later issues, when it was much more of a back and forth and trusting in each other. I think that early on Doug had every reason, either through being dictated to (although no one dictates to Doug what he should do) if he was told to hold the kid by the hand, and when he found out that's not what I needed, we nailed our working methods. Again, Doug is just phenomenal and what he did with some of those stories, I haven't read the collected versions of them in a long while, but in every issue, there was a different inker, and it wasn't until I decided that I have to ink my own work, that also was a big factor for me.

SW: When did that happen, when was that around?

BS: I think it translated into the comic books, there was a black and white special with a character with electrodes in his head and I remember Tom Palmer was inking that and Tom had to walk away from it mid-stream. I remember saying how much I wanted to ink it and I think there was that division of labour, again the first several issues in the backup of the Hulk magazine and then when it became the regular series it went from Joe Rubenstein to Bob McCloud, and Klaus Jansen, Frank Springer, so it just felt like there was this revolving door of different people coming in who were changing the way it was interpreted. So, when Tom Palmer had to walk away, I went in and lobbied to ink my own work. My inking was really sloppy at the time, and it still is I suppose at least I knew what I wanted and if I was going to make mistakes, they would be my mistakes. If I was going to drive the car off the cliff, I would rather be the one behind the wheel than a passenger. So, It was Al Milgram the editor who let me do it, he said "He has as much right to screw up his pencils as anybody else." I thought that was a great vote of confidence. After I did those issues and the final pages, I had enough confidence to come back and start doing the Morpheus issues.

Some of my most wonderful memories of Moon Knight were of cutting the zipper zone and using whiteout. Especially when they were at a Chalet, and it was snowing, and I remember feeling like I was really in that environment. I grew up in a place with a very cold environment in the winter and there was something about the winter and the silence of snowfall that could be very creepy. I enjoyed drawing those scenes and inking them the way I wanted. Like putting down spatter of white paint to be snow, it felt very visceral, but also it felt like I was a reader as much as I was the guy drawing it. When those things happen, they are too few and far between, but they make it special. So that was it when I came in with the inking style, and that set of last ten issues was great. I wish in a wired way as if issue twenty could be issue one and everything that came before that, we forgot about it. Even when I did the very first issue of the comic book run, the actual direct sales, Jim Shooter had taken such an interest in it that I redrew the entire issue to make it less like Neal. I had done some bizarre panel layouts, and Neal was known at the time for doing some really interesting panel angles, and Jim was saying 'Just tell the story'. So yeah, I ended up redrawing a good portion, if not all of it. I don't think any of those original pages have survived, but I'm reflecting on all this, and a lot was going on.

SW: The final thing for us to wrap up, you say you did the Hulk backups, and the specials and then the monthly. One of the things I love, when I go back and look at the issues and in the collected editions, is the pin-ups. There was a series of pin-ups you did, one of all the personas of Marc Spector and one of Marlene, and one of Frenchie. Firstly, were you asked to do them and was it fun to do something that was a character piece that was story based?

BS: Those, I remember they were play for me. They were pieces I needed to do for myself to break away from the influences I'd had. Plus, also to better define the characters to me, and define myself and what style I was going to be or was becoming. To me, it was playing. It was enjoyable. It was also me getting into the acting of the characters. There was one of Marlene just sort of sitting, and I remember Crawley was running with birds about, and he was just a hand-scrawled thing. I just remember feeling like I'm becoming a better storyteller and I'm getting into the acting of all the characters. Looking back at it with the benefit of hindsight, it feels like it was on the road to somewhere but at the time it felt so incremental. But they were things that I wanted to do. The way my interest manifests is that I want to run with it. I go deep and suddenly the characters don't just become characters on paper, or lines on paper, they start to have a personality and they begin to exist, for me. That was what made it such fun. That is the one thing about doing comics that I find is very different from any other form of medium. You usually work with one, or maybe two other people, but you're the director, the cinematographer, and the actors. So, to me, it wasn't until I started breaking away from the Neal Adams thing that I felt like oh, this is a David Lynch story here or a Frank Capra or Stanley Kubrick kind of moment, I started thinking more in terms of film directors.

In Scarlet that splash page of tenement buildings, I didn't want to do typical comic backgrounds. I remember one time, I was pushing everyone's buttons, and I drew some older buildings and a lamppost, and I didn't use a ruler, I did it freehand. I did all the bricks of the building freehand, and they were all loose and wonky because they felt like old buildings. To some, it was like I was breaking some core tenant of how you did backgrounds, like if it's a building you must use a ruler, but who says? It's an old building it should look like it's about to fall over, or it feels like an old lamppost. That was a big shift for me psychologically. I went from trying to draw what characters looked like to how they felt, and it was more about emotion. I wanted to draw well enough for people to be able to look at characters and say that's obviously a werewolf, that's Steven Grant, that's Marlene or whoever, and it's a passable drawing of a human being but at the same time, it's like, I found if I drew Marlene in charcoal and I smudged it for one of the pages at the end of an issue it had a different impact than if I rendered in it pen and ink. So that's when I started trying to do more technical things that would stay with me. Like ending the story on a big reveal in terms of film, like a jump scare, but in comics, it's the turning of the page. So, I remember there's one scene where Marlene is crouching with a Knife in a bathroom or something like that, and it was the last page. So, I was enjoying all of the things you could do with comic storytelling.

Whether or not it was entirely successful, I'm assuming to some extent it was. I mean Moon Knight has had how many iterations of the character? The fact that he is malleable in a weird way. I mean you can go from Bendis to Ellis and Alex Maleev, you name it, he's a fascinating character. I'm very curious to see what Marvel will do with it, but also what Disney will do with it. I mean you cannot get a better actor than Oscar Issacs. I know at the time there was sort of the wish list game that people do, should it be Keanu Reeves or Jake Gyllenhaal.

But when Oscar Issacs was announced, wow. I remember seeing him first in the Cohen Brothers film and then I saw him in Ex Machina, but also in a role with Jessica Chastain, and was like a Michael Corleone type, a younger version of Pacino, very reserved and there was an intensity to him. Yeah, this guy has the goods.

Chuck Dixon Interview

Chuck Dixon has had a massive impact on comic books since entering the industry in 1984. He joined Marvel in 1987, writing for Alien Legion, before he joined <u>Marc Spector: Moon Knight</u> in 1989. From there he has written for Batman, introducing the character Bane, as well as contributing to some of the biggest Batman events of the 1990s. He has worked for multiple other publishers creating a wealth of comics. This interview was conducted on 1 October 2021.

Scott Weatherly (SW): You are one of the longest-running contributors to Moon Knight, with 25 issues and more if you consider Marvel Knights. People talk a lot about post-2000, with Charlie Huston and beyond, and the start with Doug Moench, and that is often about it, so I'm very excited to be talking about this era. So, how were you brought in to write Moon Knight in 1989?

Chuck Dixon (CD): Well Carl Potts was assigned as editor, and I had been working on Karl's *Alien Legion* for about a year, and he liked my writing, and we got along really well. It was his idea to do away with the triple personalities and just go with Marc Spectre, Mercenary, and he thought I was best equipped to handle that angle of it. That's about as easy as it gets. An editor likes your work and hires you to write a book.

SW: Was it the same for Sal Velluto? Was he brought in, or did you bring him in?

I didn't know him at the time. It was Marvel Comics, so they were seeing portfolios all the time. Carl had seen Sal's portfolio and liked it. Carl was very much into cinematic storytelling as well as the draftsmanship you need to do comics, and he liked Sal's approach to storytelling, and so did I, so it worked out. Plus, Sal's work is somewhat more grounded in reality, which is what we were looking for.

SW: When you started working on the process, as a team, did Marvel have any directives for the series, or were you left to your own devices?

CD: Not really. I had some discussions with Carl, but I understood what he wanted. We had talked about the movie *Dogs of War (1980)*, which we both liked, and we wanted to lean into that. If anyone has seen the movie, they'll see homages to it in the first few issues of Moon Knight. There's a scene where Marc goes to see his physician, and there's a scene just like it in Dogs of War. I like the idea of this warrior character, and he goes to the doctors, and the doctors like 'You've broken this bone nine times, this bone seven ...' I thought that was really cool. I would love to do a scene with Batman like that.

SW: It is great. He gets tricked into going by Frenchie and Marlene and when the Doctor says, well you have all these scars, Marc sort of shrugs and says 'Yeah, I do'. In addition to this, you return Marc to the streets, after his time on the Avengers, but you also bring in the international elements, other than *Dogs of War*, was there anything else that inspired that?

CD: Well, since he had the mercenary background, we wanted to get him out of the United States, to third-world countries, revisiting places he had been as Marc Spectre. Most of the stories, well at least half, take place overseas.

SW: Yeah, easily about half. Visiting Burunda and the small Spanish town...

CD: Bosqueverde. Yeah, Bosqueverde is a town that only exists in Chuck Dixon comics. It's been in Air Boy, it's been in Batman, it's even been in The Simpsons.

SW: Wow, that's fantastic. As a note on that Mercenary aspect, you are one of the first to really lean into that with the book, and you dig into the life of Marc Spector, and what really comes through is this idea of consequences. The whole run seems to be about consequences, with roots back to things that have happened in the past. Was that intentional and was that what you had planned?

CD: I like deconstructed plot lines. I like when nothing ever goes right, and if the character's got a shady past it's going to impact him today. Also, this was being written when we were first starting to learn about Post Traumatic Stress Disorder and things like that. So, the idea of a soldier character being revisited by past events seemed relevant. Well, it's still relevant today, but it was new and fresh then. They weren't refereeing to it as battle fatigue anymore, they were identifying it as a lifelong issue that people that serve in combat are going to have to deal with. So, there was a lot of that.

SW: Yeah, that period of the early 90s we were also going to learn about Gulf War syndrome and other aftereffects.

CD: I had a friend who was a reporter for a newspaper, and he was doing a series of articles about Post Traumatic Stress Disorder, and it was the first time I had ever heard of it. I sort of folded that into Marc Spector's backstory.

SW: It makes total sense considering the stuff you added in. You talk about the characters that you brought back in, you brought back Bushman, a much more violent and focused version of the character. Was it intentional to bring him in first, so you could touch base with the past and launch off from that?

CD: When I take over a character, even when it's a number one, and it's a reboot or relaunch, I know Moon Knight had fans and I wanted to serve them. I'm not there to make it my Moon Knight, break everything or change everything just for the sense of change. I liked the sense of history the character had, and I wanted to use it, and long-time Moon Knight fans were happy about that.

SW: I have to say I love your version of Bushman, especially giving him his own little empire.

CD: Yeah, I wanted to make him smart too. He was kind of an imposing thug earlier, and I wanted to show this guy as having some brains behind the stuff he does.

SW: Definitely. The thing I appreciate is that, while you're not told, it is clear that he had been running Burunda for several years before we get to him. He has taken over and it's clear there is more to him than just a thug, which is a fascinating take.

CD: At the time people were still dealing with Idi Amin, and as brutal as he was, he had something going on to run that country for as long as he did, under those kinds of conditions. In creating this Thunderdome like society, you don't stay on top just by being tough you've got to be smart too.

SW: On the flip side of that you bring in another character that sits throughout your run, Jeff Wilde. He is the son of a former Moon Knight villain, Midnight Man. You say about things not going well, you really put Jeff through the wringer. What was the inspiration for bringing Jeff in and acting as a sort of sidekick?

CD: Well, they always refer to Moon Knight as Marvel's Batman, and I wanted to show why Moon Knight isn't Marvel's Batman, by bringing in a side kick and it doesn't work out. It's not a good idea, and it was sort of my comment on having a teen sidekick, to begin with. Which is ironic, as I would go on to write Batman and Robin for so long. But, yeah, I like the idea of bringing in this new character, playing with these ideas and playing with the reader's expectations. I always saw Moon Knight as his own character, not as a Marvel Batman.

SW: I think he has become very distant from that comparison now, but that was the key period when that comparison was being made, and Jeff is definitely not Robin, but he does fit into this theme of consequences. He could have been any kid, but you give him that connection. He feels like Moon Knight owes him because of what Moon Knight did to his father.

CD: Yeah, it was important to build off the past, and the sense of continuity from what had gone before.

SW: You know us comic fans, we love a bit of continuity.

CD: Oh, we love it, everything's got to interconnect. There are no strangers in comics, everyone new is connected to someone in your past, popping up again.

SW: One of the things in this run as well, is the relationship with Marlene and Frenchie. At times, it feels like a team book. Moon Knight is his own character, but he works as part of a team. Was it important to you to show that and give those characters agency?

CD: Yeah. He's a wealthy guy, and wealthy people tend to have an ensemble. The people that do the little things for them. Marc Spector isn't going to be going out and mowing the lawn, and he's a soldier so he needs technical support, that's where Frenchie comes in. So, he needs to be part of a group. He's out front, but he has people supporting him.

SW: Good point. Marlene is an interesting character for this. Not wanting to sound derogatory but she had been used as a bit of fluff in the past, but you really give her the chance to be in the thick of it and kick ass. Again, was it intentional to bring her in, in that way?

CD: I wanted him (Marc) to have a romantic interest because that is interesting, and I just tend to write that kind of female character that's stronger. That's how I initially made my name in comics, writing strong female characters, who are three-dimensional, well-rounded, and just as dangerous as the men in the story. So that was just a natural fit. I mean, Marc Spector, he's not going to be with Miss America.

SW: There are several issues in the run where she gets stuck in. Your version of Marlene is probably my favourite version of the character. As you say it would make sense that Marc would be attracted to someone that would be able to challenge him on different levels, rather than just be a beautiful woman on his arm.

CD: Yeah, he wouldn't be with a woman he had to look out for all the time. She was a badass in her own right, and that's just the kind of woman he would want to be around.

SW: You have contributed to Moon Knight and Batman in substantial ways, but when you were writing Moon Knight were there any other factors you kept in mind to make sure he was different? Or was it even a consideration in 1989?

CD: I definitely wanted to make sure he wasn't a Batman knockoff, or seen as a Batman knockoff, so I avoided any kind of... unless I was pointing out the differences, I avoided the obvious. Like, his secret identity is Marc Spector, whose just as tough as Moon Knight, quite the opposite of Bruce Wayne playing a disaffected Bertie Wooster type. I like that idea, there is no difference between the two. He had a steady female relationship and obviously didn't care for a sidekick. I also liked that, in his mind, he was pretty much Moon Knight all the time, even when he was not in costume, he was still that character.

SW: In some later issues his costume has been referred to as vestments. He is a priest or the avatar of Khonshu, he is the same person, but he has a costume for when he is in action, conducting the work of his god. Beyond the run, you also brought Moon Knight into Marvel Knights in 2000 and had him work with others like Daredevil, Punisher, Back Widow and Luke Cage. This was 10 years later, so did you come back to him with a different approach, also bringing him into a group dynamic did it change anything for you?

CD: Not really. My directive for Marvel Knights was to bring in street-level characters, as many as I could. Moon Knight seemed like a good fit and a good military fit. I had the Punisher in Marvel Knights quite a bit, but Punisher isn't really a joiner. So, he was often there more as a thorn in their side, he never became one of them. But if they needed someone with some tactical knowledge Marc Spectre was their guy.

SW: Yeah, it does feel of a piece. You can see how your run moves into Marvel Knights. One final thing and one of the things I enjoy the most is Moon Knight with some of the wider Marvel universe, Spider-man, the Punisher etc. Were there any Marvel characters you really wanted to bring in to get that relationship?

CD: Oh, I absolutely wanted the Punisher. I wanted to write Punisher so badly and this was a way of almost auditioning for what my Punisher would be like. The only regret I have is they cut my best Punisher line. There's a scene where a guy gets crushed in a car crusher and Spider-man and Moon Knight are both a little taken aback, and Punisher says, 'Yeah it's a shame what happened to that Caddy', but they (*Marvel*) cut that line, they thought it was too cruel.

SW: As a side question. I have all of *Marc Spector: Moon Knight* as issues, but it has never been collected anywhere (*at the time of this interview*). Has Marvel ever spoken to you about that, or do you know why?

CD: No, I think Marc Spector: Moon Knight is seen as sort of non-cannon like it's a departure from what had come before and what came after. So, they just sort of ignore it. Which is a bit of a problem with Marvel in general. DC digitises everything they can get their hands on; you can read pretty much everything they have ever done. However, Marvel seems to pick and choose what they digitise. It's a shame there are so many gaps, but hopefully, they will get to it.

One thing to mention that you didn't know to ask. When I was working on the book, I always told my editor, this is one of Marvel's only Jewish superheroes, why would he have the powers of an Egyptian god? I wanted to try and explain that, so it makes sense. I said maybe Khonshu isn't an Egyptian god, maybe he was a Pharoah when the Hebrews were running Egypt. So, he's actually a Hebrew figure, not an Egyptian one, but my editor at the time rejected the idea.

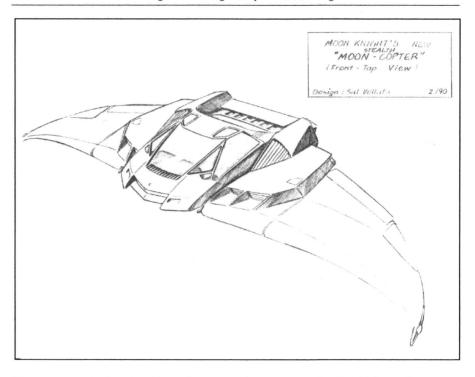

Moon-copter design for Marc Spector: Moon Knight, by Sal Velluto. From the interviewee's personal collection.

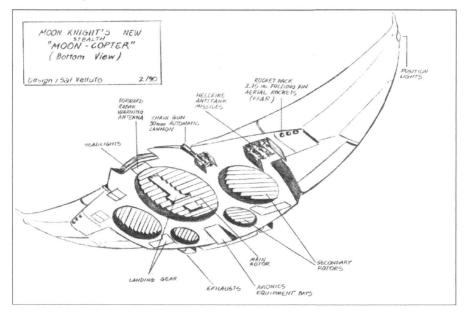

Moon-copter design for Marc Spector: Moon Knight, by Sal Velluto. From the interviewee's personal collection.

About the Contributors

Matt Corrigan co-hosts the Launchpad Podcast, a humorous look into cool nerd things like comics, movies, toys and more (launchpadpod.com, @launchpadpod). After 17 years of practical special effects, working on films like *300, Batman V. Superman*, and *Ghost Rider*, he changed careers and now teaches 5-year-olds how to read using lightsabers as pointers and with help from guest speakers like Mr. T. He won NBC's "Wipeout" and has eaten dinner sitting on California's 405 Freeway. He has a large collection of original comic art, including the David Finch Moon Knight panels printed in this book alongside his essay. Matt remembers seeing Finch's cover for *Moon Knight* Vol. 5 #6 for the first time, his true introduction to the character. His 4-year-old son Kent is every bit as nerdy as his handsome strong dad, and Matt's non-nerd wife puts up with both of them as best she can.

Brian Cronin has been writing professionally about comic books for over fifteen years now at CBR.com. He has written two books about comics for Penguin-Random House (*Was Superman a Spy? And Other Comic Book Legends Revealed* and *Why Does Batman Carry Shark Repellent? And Other Amazing Comic Book Trivia!*) and one book (*100 Things X-Men Fans Should Know & Do Before They Die*) for Triumph Books. His writing has been featured at ESPN.com, the Los Angeles Times, About.com, Vulture, the Huffington Post and Gizmodo. He features legends about entertainment and sports at his website, Legends Revealed and other pop culture features at Pop Culture References.

Jason DeHart is a passionate educator, currently teaching English at Wilkes Central High School in Wilkesboro, North Carolina. He served as a middle-grade

English teacher for eight years and an assistant professor of reading education at Appalachian State University from 2019 to 2022. DeHart uses comics in the classroom whenever possible.

Tony Farina shares his empty nest with his wife, a librarian, where they read books and watch sunsets. He has a YA book series called The Austen Chronicles from 4Horsemen Publications. He has an essay in Sequart's *Judging Dredd* collection. When not busy writing, he spends his time as a college professor with both an M.A. Ed. and an M.F.A. in Creative Writing. He hosts a weekly podcast on the Comics in Motion Podcast network where he critically analyzes indie comics and graphic novels.

Jason Kahler is a teacher, writer, and researcher from Southeast Michigan. His scholarship and creative work have appeared in *The Columbia Journal*, *Analog*, *Seneca Review*, *College English*, *How to Analyze & Review Comics* (also from Sequart), *The Stonecoast Review*, and other publications. Dr. Kahler appreciates the way Moon Knight has changed with the times and with the books' creators. He's been more than just Marvel's Batman for a long time.

Zach Katz is a writer and comic book enthusiast who graduated from Brandeis University with a degree in creative writing and anthropology. This collection is his first contribution to a project like this; however, he knows it won't be the last. His favorite phase of the moon is Waxing Crescent, unlike Marc Spector, who probably does like any of the moon phases at all.

Emmet O'Cuana is a critic and comic book writer. He was briefly tempted to take on a third persona as a cab driver, but the moment passed. He is a confirmed cat daddy and, thanks to COVID-19, recently discovered Dungeons and Dragons. He is the writer of Faraway and The Beating of Wings with Jeferson Sadzinski. He is currently working on a graphic novel set in 80's Sydney with artist Lynore Avery titled The Shadow of Night. emmetocuana.com

Jon Sapsed is a cartoonist based in England, having written and drawn stories for QueenSpark publishing and small press such as Paperjam Collective. HIs instagram is @sapsedjonathan. He also has a parallel existence as a university professor researching and publishing on the creative industries. He is Co-Editor of the Oxford Handbook of Creative Industries. HIs twitter is @jsapsed. He has been following Moon Knight comics since the 1980s.

Leyna Vincent is one of the alters in the DID (dissociative identity disorder) system of Douglas J. Vincent. We were first diagnosed with DID in 2004, after about 10 years of being misdiagnosed. In 2016, I/we decided to start sharing our life story online, to help educate and raise awareness about DID, because it is a very misunderstood and stigmatized disorder. A few years later, I became interested in Moon Knight, because of his connection to DID. I started learning more about that character and decided to use Moon Knight as a focus for our DID education and awareness efforts. This has led to opportunities such as becoming the DID consultant for Jed MacKay, the current writer of the Moon Knight comics for Marvel. I also collaborate with Gamma Charge: The Strongest Podcast There Is, giving my feedback about the representation of DID in Hulk comic books. We live in the Midwest region of the United States and enjoy writing, drawing and reading in our spare time.

Scott Weatherly started his Sequart journey by editing and overseeing his first essay collection, *Judging Dredd*. He can also be found chatting about pop culture and history on his podcasts 20th Century Geek and Stories out of Time and Space. Among all this, he enjoys living in a rural village in Derbyshire with his wife, daughter and dog. Scott has been a travelling companion of Moon Knight since the early 2000s and wants to make more people aware of how great the character is.

ALSO FROM **SEQUART**

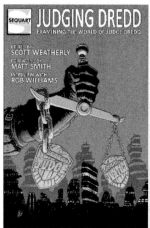  

JUDGING DREDD: EXAMINING THE WORLD OF JUDGE DREDD
HOW TO ANALYZE & REVIEW COMICS: A HANDBOOK ON COMICS CRITICISM
THE BRITISH INVASION: ALAN MOORE, NEIL GAIMAN, GRANT MORRISON, AND THE
    INVENTION OF THE MODERN COMIC BOOK WRITER

MUSINGS ON MONSTERS: OBSERVATIONS ON THE WORLD OF CLASSIC HORROR
FROM BAYOU TO ABYSS: EXAMINING JOHN CONSTANTINE, HELLBLAZER
CLASSICS ON INFINITE EARTHS: THE JUSTICE LEAGUE AND DC CROSSOVER CANON

BOOKS ON SCI-FI FRANCHISES:

UNAUTHORIZED OFFWORLD ACTIVATION: EXPLORING THE STARGATE FRANCHISE

SOMEWHERE BEYOND THE HEAVENS: EXPLORING BATTLESTAR GALACTICA

THE CYBERPUNK NEXUS: EXPLORING THE BLADE RUNNER UNIVERSE

THE SACRED SCROLLS: COMICS ON THE PLANET OF THE APES

BRIGHT LIGHTS, APE CITY: EXAMINING THE PLANET OF THE APES MYTHOS

NEW LIFE AND NEW CIVILIZATIONS: EXPLORING STAR TREK COMICS

A LONG TIME AGO: EXPLORING THE STAR WARS CINEMATIC UNIVERSE

A GALAXY FAR, FAR AWAY: EXPLORING STAR WARS COMICS

A MORE CIVILIZED AGE: EXPLORING THE STAR WARS EXPANDED UNIVERSE

THE WEIRDEST SCI-FI COMIC EVER MADE: UNDERSTANDING JACK KIRBY'S *2001: A SPACE ODYSSEY*

BOOKS ON GRANT MORRISON:

GRANT MORRISON: THE EARLY YEARS

OUR SENTENCE IS UP: SEEING GRANT MORRISON'S *THE INVISIBLES*

CURING THE POSTMODERN BLUES: READING GRANT MORRISON AND CHRIS WESTON'S *THE FILTH* IN THE 21ST CENTURY

THE ANATOMY OF ZUR-EN-ARRH: UNDERSTANDING GRANT MORRISON'S BATMAN

BOOKS ON WARREN ELLIS:

SHOT IN THE FACE: A SAVAGE JOURNEY TO THE HEART OF *TRANSMETROPOLITAN*

KEEPING THE WORLD STRANGE: A *PLANETARY* GUIDE

VOYAGE IN NOISE: WARREN ELLIS AND THE DEMISE OF WESTERN CIVILIZATION

WARREN ELLIS: THE CAPTURED GHOSTS INTERVIEWS

ON TV AND MOVIES:

MUTANT CINEMA: THE X-MEN TRILOGY FROM COMICS TO SCREEN

GOTHAM CITY 14 MILES: 14 ESSAYS ON WHY THE 1960S BATMAN TV SERIES MATTERS

IMPROVING THE FOUNDATIONS: *BATMAN BEGINS* FROM COMICS TO SCREEN

WHY DO WE FALL?: EXAMINING CHRISTOPHER NOLAN'S *THE DARK KNIGHT TRILOGY*

TIME IS A FLAT CIRCLE: EXAMINING *TRUE DETECTIVE*, SEASON ONE

OTHER BOOKS:

HUMANS AND PARAGONS: ESSAYS ON SUPER-HERO JUSTICE

MOVING PANELS: TRANSLATING COMICS TO FILM

THE MIGNOLAVERSE: HELLBOY AND THE COMICS ART OF MIKE MIGNOLA

MOVING TARGET: THE HISTORY AND EVOLUTION OF GREEN ARROW

TEENAGERS FROM THE FUTURE: ESSAYS ON THE LEGION OF SUPER-HEROES

THE BEST THERE IS AT WHAT HE DOES: EXAMINING CHRIS CLAREMONT'S X-MEN

AND THE UNIVERSE SO BIG: UNDERSTANDING *BATMAN: THE KILLING JOKE*

THE DEVIL IS IN THE DETAILS: EXAMINING MATT MURDOCK AND DAREDEVIL

MINUTES TO MIDNIGHT: TWELVE ESSAYS ON *WATCHMEN*

WHEN MANGA CAME TO AMERICA: SUPER-HERO REVISIONISM IN *MAI, THE PSYCHIC GIRL*

THE FUTURE OF COMICS, THE FUTURE OF MEN: MATT FRACTION'S *CASANOVA*

DOCUMENTARY FILMS:

DIAGRAM FOR DELINQUENTS

SHE MAKES COMICS

THE IMAGE REVOLUTION

NEIL GAIMAN: DREAM DANGEROUSLY

GRANT MORRISON: TALKING WITH GODS

WARREN ELLIS: CAPTURED GHOSTS

COMICS IN FOCUS: CHRIS CLAREMONT'S X-MEN

For more information and for exclusive content, visit Sequart.org.

Printed in Great Britain
by Amazon